Love

Your

Husband

DISCIPLESHIP
PUBLICATIONS
INTERNATIONAL

Love

Gloria E. Baird
Kay S. McKean

Your

Husband

Needs unconditional acceptance

Love Your Husband
© 2001 by Discipleship Publications International
2 Sterling Road, Billerica, Mass. 01862

Printed in the United States of America

All Scripture quotations, unless indicated, are taken from the HOLY BIBLE, NEW INTERNATIONAL VERSION. Copyright © 1973, 1978, 1984 by the International Bible Society. Used by permission of Zondervan Publishing House. All rights reserved.

The "NIV" and "New International Version" trademarks are registered in the United States Patent Trademark Office by the International Bible Society. Use of either trademark requires the permission of the International Bible Society.

Cover and Book Design: Christine Nolan
Image © 2001, FPG International, LLC.

ISBN: 1-57782-154-8

To Al Baird, my husband and best friend,
With you my life is an exciting adventure.

To my husband, Randall Kent McKean,
I only have eyes for you.

Contents

Introduction

KSM

> Likewise, teach the older women to be reverent in the way they live...to teach what is good. Then they can train the younger women to love their husbands and children.
>
> Titus 2:3-4

I am an older woman. Editor, please make sure that "er" is in there. I said older, not old. This "older" thing is, at times, very hard for me to accept. In my heart, I'm still a kid. I am still learning, growing, changing. I am still insecure at times and even uncertain of myself. I thought older women always had it all together, always knew exactly what to do and how to do it. But here I am, in that "older woman" category, and having to become all that it involves.

We older married women are a unique and, if I may say so, very valuable group. We are women who have been around the block a few times. We are women who have raised children and sent them out into the world. We have been married for at least a couple of decades. We remember the Monkees and record players, Carnaby Street and Woodstock. Some of us really did say, "Groovy." We know where we were when Kennedy was shot, and we stopped everything to watch the first man walk on the moon. We worried over Vietnam and the Cold War. We have a thing or two to say.

What does God tell older women to do with their lives? Lots of things, but in particular, we are commissioned to train younger women. We are called to train them to love God and to become more Christlike. We are especially commanded to train women to love their husbands, and that is what we are endeavoring to do in this book.

Gloria and I are putting our heads together, and from this wealth of experience—victory and failure, laughter and tears, better and worse—we are going to share with you some of what we have learned. We have each chosen topics that are dear to our hearts, and we look forward to training you to love your husbands in better and richer ways. We hope that new brides, middle-aged wives and even those celebrating their golden wedding anniversaries will benefit from the words we write. Our desire is for all of us to become the wives God has called us to be and for our changes to produce happy and grateful husbands.

Gloria has been an older woman a little bit longer than I have. (Again—older, not old!) I have been blessed to have already learned so much from her training me to love my husband. So it is a pleasure, although a bit perplexing, to be in the same category with her. It is an honor to work on this project with her. As always, I am delighted to be a writer for Discipleship Publications International, and I especially thank Sheila Jones for working with us, sorting out our thoughts, and bringing together what we hope will be a book that glorifies God.

It is remarkable when husbands and wives love each other and stay together through thick and thin. Happy families, faithful marriages, loving spouses— these are not reserved for fairy tales and fantasy lives; they describe the lives of all couples who die to themselves and live their lives God's way.

Kay S. McKean
March 2001

GEB

God answers our prayers in unusual ways. As a young bride in the traditional church, I longed for some practical, spiritual training from older women. I remember asking the elders' wives to teach a class for the younger women, but they felt unequipped. I knew Titus 2:3-4, and somehow the preacher teaching the"Ladies' Bible Class" did not seem to fulfill that scripture or meet my needs. At that time I could think of only three older women (my mother being one) who were attempting to put that scripture into practice. Feeling the need in my own life moved me to pray to become an older woman who would be willing to teach and train younger women. Never would I have dreamed that part of God's answer to that prayer would include my coauthoring a book!

So now, I am an older woman. I admit it and, believe it or not, I am very happy to be at this stage of life (considering the alternatives!). However, writing a book seemed out of my league. Kay is an author (and she has the book to prove it[1]); I am the one who would rather teach ten classes than write one chapter! God does have a sense of humor. He seems to delight in putting us in situations where we know that we must rely on him. There are times when you just simply know that you need to respond to a challenge—this was one of those times for me. Having three married daughters (and now six granddaughters) motivated me to want to share the things God has taught me about loving my husband. That motivation was heightened when I thought of the many more daughters and granddaughters in God's family who need to be trained to love their husbands and future husbands.

I love marriage—actually, Al Baird is the reason for that. Because of his love for God and his love for me, it has been easier for me to love my husband. I admire Randy and Kay's marriage; they have a great friendship and a great family. They and we have worked on our marriages for years with God's help and with the help of many others. Most of what we have to share about marriage comes from the "school of hard knocks"—either hard knocks that we have experienced ourselves or the "bumps" and difficulties of couples we have counseled. Life teaches so many lessons; some are very painful. You cannot bypass the value of days, months and years in the learning process. That is why Titus 2:4 makes so much sense. Older women have lived longer, made more mistakes, and hopefully accumulated wisdom. It is only fitting that, with God's help, we should share what we've learned with others.

As Kay and I worked together on this book, we selected various topics that have been vital and helpful to our marriages, realizing we could not cover every need. I especially want to acknowledge the tremendous help we got from Sheila Jones from start to finish. She gave input about the subject matter, helped set our goals and edited to make our work even better. I am very thankful for the spiritual support given by Sheila and the group of women who were praying continually as we were writing.

It is our prayer that this book will be a springboard to stimulate you to read more, learn more, pray more and do more—to love your husband better than ever—to the glory of God.

Gloria E. Baird
March 2001

NOTES

1. Kay Summers McKean, *Our Beginning: Genesis Through the Eyes of a Woman* (Billerica, Mass: Discipleship Publications International, 1996).

Remember Your Vow

 KSM

> "...to have and to hold
> from this day forward
> till death do us part."

I love weddings. I love getting dressed up and going to the ceremony, seeing the happy faces and the decorations of flowers and ribbons, and feeling the excitement in the air. Every bride is beautiful, and every groom is a pleasure to watch as he sees his beloved come down that aisle. In the midst of the songs and the satin, the romance and the rings, something mysterious and poignant occurs: the marriage vows. They may be modern or old-fashioned, personalized or repeated, but they always are a declaration of one thing:

> A man and a woman are promising before God and witnesses to be committed to this relationship for the rest of their lives.

Promise, vow, covenant—whichever word you use, the meaning is the same. It is an exchange, an agreement between two entities that is binding and will never be forgotten. When this agreement is between two people, each person must be true to that which has been stated and expected.

A God of Promises

Promises are very big things to God. They are important to him because he is a God of promises. From the beginning of time, God has made covenants with his people that he has been faithful to fulfill. He promised Noah that he would save him and his family through the flood, and he did (Genesis 6). He made a covenant, with a sign of the rainbow, that he would not wipe out the world with water again (Genesis 9). His covenant with Abraham led to the birth of a nation (Genesis 15). His covenant with the Israelites brought forth the law and eventually a land they could call home (Exodus 19). On and on he made and kept promises, leading up to the greatest and best promise of all: eternal life. Jesus showed us this promise as he drank the cup at his last supper: "This is my blood of the covenant" (Matthew 26:28). The covenant of Jesus' blood is God's vow to us that through the death of

Jesus, we can have forgiveness of sins. We stake our faith, our very lives, on a promise from God. Without that promise, where would we be?

Promises We Make

As God's children, we make promises too. However, many of our promises are made without thought and seldom kept: "I promise to write you, call you, pray for you." "I vow to stay on my diet, save money, study hard." But there is one vow that is truly the most important one we will ever make and that should never be taken lightly: the vow to make Jesus the Lord of our lives. When we declare that we want Jesus as our Savior and Lord and then we follow through with baptism for the forgiveness of our sins, we are entering into a covenant relationship with God himself. God is promising to be with us, to give us his Holy Spirit, to forgive us of all our sins, and to bring us to live with him forever in heaven. We are promising that we will love God with all our heart, serving him and obeying him to the best of our ability, until the day we die. What an exciting covenant God has allowed us to share with him!

The second most important vow we can make is the vow of marriage. We are entering into a covenant with a man that will last until death. We are promising this man that we will love and honor him, be faithful to him, and stick by him in all circumstances. We are not only promising this to our new husband, but to God himself. And God is not taking our words lightly.

In fact, God is not pleased if we speak about important things in a casual or thoughtless manner. Consider these scriptures to see God's heart concerning the vows we make:

> When a man makes a vow to the Lord or takes an oath to obligate himself by a pledge, he must not break his word but must do everything he said. (Numbers 30:2)

> If you make a vow to the Lord your God, do not be slow to pay it, for the Lord your God will certainly demand it of you and you will be guilty of sin. But if you refrain from making a vow, you will not be guilty. Whatever your lips utter you must be sure to do, because you made your vow freely to the Lord your God with your own mouth. (Deuteronomy 23:21-23)

> When you make a vow to God, do not delay in fulfilling it. He has no pleasure in fools; fulfill your vow. It is better not to vow than to make a vow and not fulfill it....Therefore stand in awe of God. (Ecclesiastes 5:4-5, 7)

How different that is from the way most people view vows today. For so many, the attitude is *I promise this, but if it doesn't work out, or if it's hard, or inconvenient, I'll back out.* In the world today we hear young women say, "I want to get married" and then quickly add, "but if I run into problems, I can always get divorced." We hear in the news about couples on their second, third or fourth marriage, and it is blithely accepted as a fact of life. Our society has a low level of commitment to anything, let alone God or marriage.

On the contrary, as disciples, we are women of our word. We say what we mean and we mean what we say. We meant it when we said, "Jesus is Lord," and we meant it when we said, "Till death do us part." Feelings come and go. Commitment remains.

My Own Vows

I said my vows on a warm summer evening in 1977. The church sanctuary was candlelit and filled with the fragrance of roses and gardenias. The songs included "You and I" by Stevie Wonder and "Color My World" by Chicago. In that setting, among family and friends, I promised to make Randy my lawfully wedded husband. It was not a difficult promise to make; I did not struggle, waver or hesitate. I was madly, deeply, truly in love; and I was thrilled to become Mrs. Randy McKean.

Through nearly a quarter century of marriage, I have been dedicated to being Randy's wife. It has been a fun, exciting, fulfilling and wonderful adventure. But there were times when the feelings waned, the excitement faded and the passion cooled. Through babies and sicknesses and career challenges and moves and deaths of family members and simple differences of opinion, there were times when we did not operate as "one" but rather as two disconnected individuals.

Thankfully, God had not forgotten the promise we made to each other—nor would he let us forget it. That promise always drew us back to each other, and we would fan into flame those coals of commitment again and again.

There is an Asian proverb that states, "No one can say of his house, 'There is no trouble here.'" Indeed, I have yet to meet a couple married more than a month who has not run into some kind of problem in their relationship. Yet there is such a freedom and relief in knowing that our marriages do not have to depend on circumstances or feelings. When a wife knows in her heart that for her, there is never a back door, then she can joyfully and completely love her husband in the way that God intended.

I remember learning the Ten Commandments when I was a little girl. When we got to the one that said, "That shalt not covet thy neighbour's wife" (Exodus 20:17 KJV), I asked my mother what the word "covet" meant. I learned that to covet meant to want something that did not belong to me. God had already said not to take what did not belong to us ("Thou shalt not steal." "Thou shalt not commit adultery."), now he was saying, "Don't even want it!" It is not only men who might have a wandering eye; women also can be given to fantasize about other men. They could wonder, "What if I'd married the other guy?" For example, if a wife views her husband as irresponsible, overweight or uncommunicative, she might have a tendency to look for a way out or to find someone better. The world certainly encourages us to bail out when things get uncomfortable or unpleasant. But a Christian woman will be loyal and mature enough to keep her promise to her husband, not only in body but also in heart.

Love in marriage is inspired by our commitment to the vow we made on our wedding day. As you continue through the following chapters of this book, you will see many issues being addressed in order to help you to love your husband. With every challenge, every need, every conviction, every piece of advice, know that God is saying, "Remember your vow." Truly, he remembers it well himself, and will never forget.

INTO YOUR HEART

1. Think back to your wedding day. Place yourself standing in front of your handsome husband-to-be, looking into his eyes, and making your vows to him. If you have an audio or video tape of your wedding, replay your vows to freshen your memory.

2. How are you doing in being faithful to those vows—not just on the outside, but down deep in your heart?

3. Plan a special romantic time with your husband in which you restate your vows to him. If you feel resistant to this suggestion, check your heart: are you willing to be vulnerable, supportive and submissive in your relationship with your husband? If not, pray to change, get help and then change—for your sake, his sake, your children's sakes and God's sake.

4. Remember times in your life when you decided to keep your vow even though it was difficult. How did God grow your character and your relationship during these times?

5. Write any other response to this chapter and commitments you want to make.

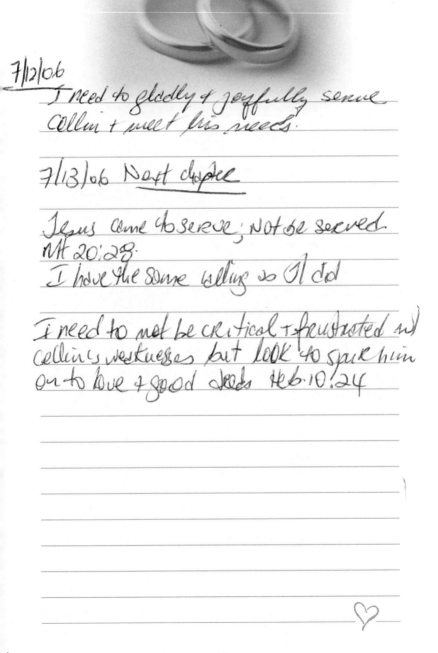

7/12/06

I need to gladly & joyfully serve
Collin & meet his needs.

7/13/06 Next chapter

Jesus came to serve, Not be served.
Mt 20:28.
I have the same calling as He did

I need to not be critical + frustrated w/
Collins weaknesses but look to spur him
on to love + good deeds Heb. 10:24

♡

23

A Suitable Helper

Trusting God
Surrender

♡ KSM

> The Lord God said, "It is not good for the man to be alone.
> I will make a helper suitable for him."
>
> *Genesis 2:18*

This chapter is all about a five-letter word called "trust." It's not about trusting me, or even about trusting your husband. It's about trusting God. This chapter takes us to a place that can be difficult for us because it involves our futures, our dreams and our very lives.

It takes trust to initially give our lives to God and become disciples—to say to God, "I'll go anywhere, do anything, give up everything for you." It takes trust to live our lives day to day following Jesus—being willing to change, to grow, to learn, to stretch, to repent often. And it takes trust to be able to look at the man you love, the man you have chosen to be your husband, and say, "I want to be a suitable helper for you."

All of these things are challenging because they require us to give up what is most precious in our lives: ourselves. We cling to our selfish natures and our self-will for dear life, believing that if we let go of them, our lives will fall apart, and we will be left empty-handed and desolate. Yet this call to surrender is exactly what is needed—not only to live our lives fully as disciples of Jesus, but also to have marriages that are complete, whole and satisfying—the way God planned marriages to be.

Man and Woman Are God's Creation

In the beginning, God created this world we live in. He made the sun and the moon, and he gave a name to each of the stars. He separated the waters from the sky and gathered the water together to produce dry ground. He allowed for vegetation and placed every creature in its proper place. For his coup de grace he created a man. As he put his finishing touches on his universe, he recognized that all he made was good. That is, until he came to the man, at which point he said, "It is *not* good for the man to be alone" (Genesis 2:18, emphasis added). There was one element missing to make his entire creation complete, and that element was a woman. Once that part of the puzzle had been added, God looked at all he had made and noted that it was "very good" (Genesis 1:31).

A popular book today describes men and women as being from two different planets, but the Bible reminds us that not only are we from the same planet, but we are also made by the same creator from the same dust in the ground. I can agree that sometimes the ways men and women think and communicate seem light-years apart. (See chapter 4 where Gloria points out some of the differences.) But we must also recognize the similarities that we have: the needs to be loved, to be respected and to be affirmed. *to make stronger* Understanding these common needs enables us to learn how to fulfill the role that God has called us to as wives: becoming suitable helpers for our husbands.

It is at this point that I'd like for you, the reader, to stop and reflect on this. Ask yourself: "Do I see myself *yep* as the one person in this world who can make my husband complete?" If you do see yourself as that person, *yep* does it make you happy? Or do you feel frustrated, *Praying to really digest this* wishing that he were the one to make you complete? Again, remember that the theme of this chapter is trust. Do you really trust that if you are striving to be all you can be for your husband, then God will make you all you were created to be? These are questions not to be taken lightly. The answers can and will determine the success of your marriage.

Stand By Your Man?

When I was a little girl, my friends and I would play a game counting the buttons on our blouses and skirts. Each button represented a man of a certain occupation: "Doctor, lawyer, businessman, thief, butcher, baker, Indian chief." (Native American did not rhyme—sorry!) Whoever was named when a girl ran out of buttons, was the type of man she would marry. It was just a game, but in a sense we defined ourselves by our future husbands! In the same way, many of the adult women I looked up to were defined in terms of the man with whom they were partnered. "Mrs. Stone? Oh yes, she's the doctor's wife." "Mrs. Brady? Isn't she the plumber's wife?" All of the television sitcom wives portrayed characters that did nothing but get into trouble while their husbands were out working at the "real" jobs.

Women my age and younger began to resist this image of womanhood, and rightfully so. We did not want to be defined by a man. We wanted to be independent and self-sufficient. We agreed with a very popular feminist of our time, who said, "A woman without a man is like a fish without a bicycle!" We could bring home the bacon and fry it up in a pan; we could roar; we had numbers too big to ignore! This attitude, blossoming in my generation and intensifying through the following decades, had some merit. The problem occurred, and still occurs, when these philosophies exist to further our own selfish ends. When God is left out of the picture, women become angry and spiteful. Their attitude toward men becomes demeaning and condescending. This pendulum swing brings a wrecking ball to a marriage.

Only God has the perfect answer and the perfect balance. Women are to find their identity and completeness through a relationship with him. God will use any woman, married or single, when she is surrendered to his will. For the married woman, God's will is that she commit herself daily to helping her husband in any way she can. Other than her relationship with God, her relationship with her husband is to be her number one priority. Just as she studies the Bible to learn about God and how to please him, she must study her husband in order to meet his needs. Her identity is not lost in the process, but rather God will use this process to enable her to become all he has created her to be. She must trust that God will work through her surrender.

God Will Do Great Things

Think of some of the heroines of the Bible. Noah's wife probably never dreamed of living in a floating zoo, but because she helped her husband to obey God's commands, she and her family were saved from devastation. (Read Genesis 6-9.) Sarah traveled to unknown lands with her husband and so became the mother of the Israelite nation. God's plan for Abraham was not for him alone, but specifically for Sarah. She "found herself" through her submission to her husband. (Read Genesis 15-21 and 1 Peter 3:5-6.) Esther protected the Israelite nation from annihilation by being a good wife to an impulsive king; the Jews still celebrate her memory at the feast of Purim. (Read the book of Esther.) Rahab changed her career, her religion and her culture when she married Salmon; many generations later King David and Jesus the Messiah came from that union. (Read Joshua 6:22-25.) In the same way, Ruth gave up everything to become the wife of Boaz, and God blessed her also to be a direct ascendant of David and Jesus. (Read the book of Ruth.)

Note that each of these women, and many more, were used greatly not because of their faith in their husbands, but because of their faith in God. They did what was right toward their husbands because of their submission to God. These are the examples that we must follow. If we believe in God, if we believe his words in the Bible, we will be suitable helpers for our husbands, and God will bless us in the process.

For some women the choice to be a suitable helper may mean changing a career, moving to a faraway location, or making other equally dramatic adjustments. But for most women, being a suitable helper is simply understanding the daily needs of her husband and adapting to those needs. It means learning what foods he likes and deciding to learn how to cook them (or at least where to order them for take-out!). It means keeping the house the way he likes it. It means dressing to please him and making him proud of you. It means being a woman who makes him want to be a better man.

Are these suggestions so difficult? Yet some women balk at them and insist on having things their own way. "No man is going to tell me how to…" I am saying that it is not a man that is giving these "suggestions," it is God. If we cannot do these small things to please our husbands, how on earth can we do the bigger and ultimately more important things?

I never had a goal to be a preacher's wife. In fact, as a child, my idea of a preacher's wife was someone who was mousy and frumpy, someone without a whole lot to say, whose main contribution was to bake cookies and sit alone in the front pew during church. When I became a disciple, my ideas changed considerably because I saw women in the church who were dynamic and forceful—and married to the ministers. But I still didn't think that was for me! I wanted to serve God in any capacity, but my dreams and goals were in a different direction than being a part of a church staff.

Well, you can guess what happened. God arranged for me to fall in love with a wonderful, godly young man who desired with all of his heart to be in the ministry. I made the decision that I would follow his lead and give my heart to his dreams. Because of that decision, I believe that God has blessed my life in ways beyond my wildest imagination. The things we have been able to do, the people we have been blessed to know, the places God has taken us have far outweighed my meager ambitions. I also believe that because of my choice, God has brought out talents and capabilities in me that I did not know I possessed. But I must confess this: there have been times that I have "bucked the system"—God's system. I have wanted to change directions, to give up, to say, "It's my turn." Several times I have had to remind myself of my commitment—first to God, and then to my husband. My willingness to be a helper for my husband is fueled only by my trust in God.

The choice we make to be a suitable helper to our husbands does not mean that God will make it easy on us. No matter what adjustments we make in order to do this, there will be many times when we must simply trust God with our direction in life. This does not mean that we have no say in decisions or that we should blindly allow our husbands to take us down paths that we know are dangerous, as will be discussed in other chapters of this book. But it does mean that in order to have a successful marriage, we must discover ways to enable our husbands to be the men God created them to be.

Our husbands will never be perfect men, any more than we will be perfect women. Too often though, wives see weaknesses in their husbands and become critical and irritated instead of considering how to "spur [them] on toward love and good deeds" (Hebrews 10:24). To be a helper involves creativity. If you want your family to have regular family devotionals, but your husband has not made the time for that, then use common sense and innovation to help your husband find the time. If your finances are out of control, figure out how you can keep a budget and have a plan to help get out of debt. Don't nag, but cooperate with your husband and help him to know that you are on his side! These are just small examples of ways you can make a difference in your marriage. Remember that God created you with the capability of being a helper. The world may look down on the role of "helper," but it is the highest calling according to the one who said that he "did not come to be served, but to serve" (Matthew 20:28).

This chapter began with an admonition to trust. Placing our lives and all we hold dear before our husbands requires an ample helping of trust. But we must remember that the trust goes both ways: God is entrusting you with this man—your husband. God is trusting that you will love him, be kind to him, serve him and meet his needs. God is trusting that you will be the wife that he created you to be. That man—the one that you sleep with and eat with and share a bathroom with and fuss over bills with—is a man that God loves fiercely. That is why God has put you in his life. God trusts you.

The knowledge of this fact should make us want to live up to that trust and be all we can be for our husbands. It should inspire us to give up our selfishness and willfulness and love our husbands fully. If God can trust us to be suitable helpers for our men, then nothing can stop us from having marriages that bring glory to him and joy to our own lives. We can look at our lives and look at our husbands and agree with God: "It is very good!"

INTO YOUR HEART

1. Is there anything in your life that you are unwilling to "let go of" for God? If so, what? Why is it difficult for you to trust him in your surrender?

2. Is there anything in your life that you are unwilling to "let go of" for your husband? If so, what? Why is it difficult for you to trust God in your surrender to your husband? *No. I am praying that this is revealed to me.*

3. What does it mean to you that you are your husband's helper, that you make him complete? *I help him in complement everything. I make him to him to greater. for God.*

4. Even though you and your husband are very different, how are you alike? *Both him + love God. Created like God.*

5. What does it mean to you to know that God trusts you to be a suitable helper to your man...to love him, serve him and seek to meet his needs?

6. Write any other response to this chapter and commitments you want to make.

5. God trusts that I can ☐. He allowed Collin to be w/ me. He sees my weaknesses + struggles + God has the faith that I will ☐ to fit the role that he has for me as a wife of his son, Collin.

4. Alike
- we think thru the details, think ahead, plan things.
- Serving + encouraging others, strive to be helpful.
- always do our best at all that we do.

<u>3/8/03</u> I am praying to embrace the role of a suitable helper, but I must admit that sometimes I feel like the slave. Thru out all my feelings I need to persevere, exhibit mercy + grace. I need to fix my eyes on JJ. He came to serve + not to be served. This is the role God mapped out 4 me. I will be happy if I live it out + not fight it.

♡

3/23/03 God, when he created the earth, he saw that it was good. Everything was good, except when it came to man. It is is not good for man to be alone. After the creation of woman, God saw it was very good. God, not good to very good and it involved the creation of woman.

— I need to encourage Collin, a lot more.
— Needs of Collin; Needs to be Respected, Needs to be loved, needs to be made stronger (affirmed).
— Study Collin out in order to meet his needs

* God loves Collin intensely & he trusts me to love Collin, be kind to him, build him up, & be the wife I need to be for him. God is trusting me w/ Collin, his son.

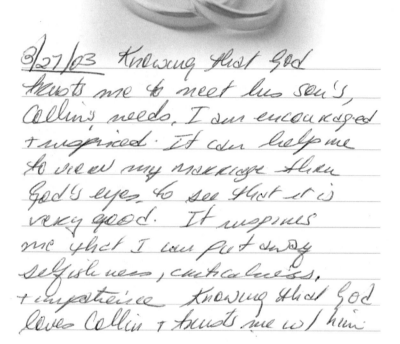

8/27/03 Knowing that God trusts me to meet his son's, Collin's needs, I am encouraged + inspired. It can help me to view my marriage thru God's eyes, to see that it is very good. It inspires me that I can put away selfishness, criticalness, + impatience knowing that God loves Collin + trusts me w/ him.

I have the same task as J. J came to serve + not be served. As my husband's helper, my role is to serve + not concentrate on being served; or worrying about who will take care of me.

♡

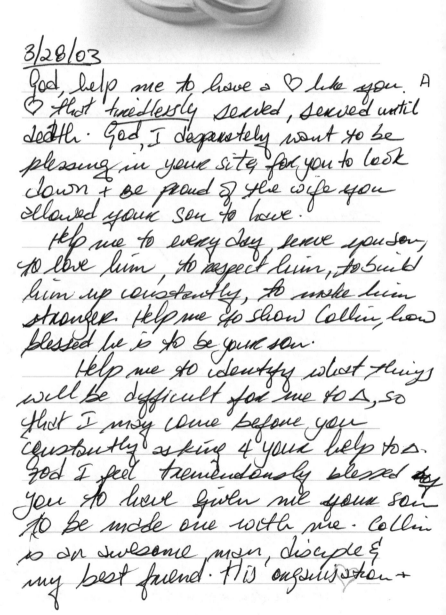

3/28/03

God, help me to have a ♡ like you. A ♡ that tirelessly served, served until death. God, I desperately want to be pleasing in your sight, for you to look down + be proud of the wife you allowed your son to have.

Help me to every day serve your son, to love him, to respect him, to build him up constantly, to make him stronger. Help me to show Collin, how blessed he is to be your son.

Help me to identify what things will be difficult for me to △, so that I may come before you constantly asking 4 your help to △. God I feel tremendously blessed by you to have given me your son to be made one with me. Collin is an awesome man, disciple & my best friend. His organization +

depth of thinking inspires me, his ♡ of getting things done encourages me + his patience + love for me floors me.

Help me father to put aside my impatience + Replace it father with patience, grace + mercy. Please replace my criticalness w/ love, under-standi innovation + maturity to help in all situations.

Help me above all else, I think to always + to deepen my understanding of the role of a wife you, God, has designed it. Help me to love, appreciate, be excited + embrace the role of a helper, lover, inspirer, friend, one who shows respect 4 her husband and one who is gentle. Thank you, father for such a clear cut role. There is not confusion the bible says it all.

Love, Lynelle

42

Adult to Adult

Being Honest.
Speaking the truth in love.
Take responsibility of my actions

"I feel like I have three children—my two little ones and my husband!! I am constantly picking up after him, and he never seems to remember where he puts anything. It's hard being the only adult in our house!" *I understand this.*

"My husband gives me play-by-play instructions for everything I do; I'm not sure I could do much without him. He often says he has taught me everything I know. It reminds me of the way my father treated me."

Marriages come in all different shapes and sizes. Husbands and wives have unique backgrounds, personalities, strengths and weaknesses. Because of the many variables, the meshing of two lives is quite an adventure. In fact, it is nothing short of a miracle. God's plan is amazing, and only as we follow that plan will our marriages be successful. From the beginning God saw that it was not good for man to be alone, so God made a helper suitable for him

(Genesis 2:18). By God's design he made woman from man's rib—from his side (Genesis 2:22). The very first marriage was husband and wife—side by side—adult to adult.

In today's world most marriages have veered way off track from God's design. Many times our role models have been anything but godly. We have seen the overpowering patriarch: the husband and father who causes everyone to cower before him. We have seen the controlling matriarch: the wife and mother who "rules the roost" and calls the shots. And we have seen everything in between. Without even realizing it, we imitate these examples around us, whether good or bad.

It is helpful to step back and take an objective look at the interactions in our marriages. Psychologist Eric Berne developed an interesting theory of interpersonal relationships known as Transactional Analysis. According to his theory, we function and interact with each other in one of three different ways:

> Parent to Child
>
> Child to Parent
>
> Adult to Adult

A relationship between two adults will be unhealthy if one functions as the parent and the other as the child. Only when we relate adult to adult will our interactions be fulfilling. It is faith-building to remember that God's plan from the beginning was that we, as husband and wife, function side by side, adult to adult.

Don't Be Your Husband's Mother

The mothering instinct is often strong in us as women. This instinct is God-given for the relationship of a mother with her child, but not for the relationship of a wife with her husband. You may be saying, "Well, my husband acts like a child, so that's why I treat him the way I do!" or "Someone has to be mature around our house!" Whatever your reasoning is, it looks bad, sounds bad and is bad when you treat your husband as a child! It is not God's design. Somehow, wives can too easily get a "my way is best" and "I know best" attitude.

Al still teases me about one of our first bumps as newlyweds moving into our apartment. He was unpacking dishes and putting them into the kitchen cabinet. In some not-so-subtle ways I let him know the kitchen was my domain. We can laugh about it now, but it wasn't very funny then. Could it be that I thought I knew best? Al has never wanted to take over the kitchen, but it would have been a smoother move if I had been humble.

It seems to me that wives are usually more critical of husbands than vice versa. We can be very "picky" about minor things. Have you ever observed a wife correcting her husband again and again, sometimes mercilessly? She usually comes off looking a lot worse than he does, even though he is doing something that she thinks is wrong or annoying.

I have a vivid memory of being in a group when I corrected a small detail of something Al was saying. The other men in the group immediately reacted by rolling their eyes and making faces. I was defenseless, and I still remember the pain of the moment. Our criticalness and "mothering" often turns into a bossy and even nagging tone as we work hard to get our points across. We need to be reminded of Solomon's words: "A quarrelsome wife is like a constant dripping" (Proverbs 19:13). Not exactly an endearing description!!

NO— Don't Be Your Husband's Child

In some marriages the interactions may go in the other direction with the wife being in the child role. The husband may be very controlling or demanding; the wife may be trying to keep the peace or avoiding taking responsibility. Patterns start early in marriage with each of us bringing our own background and "baggage" into the mix. And that baggage has much to do with the dynamics in our family backgrounds. A wife's immaturity or irresponsibility may elicit a strong parental response from her husband. Some husbands are so controlling that they intimidate their wives into a childlike cowering or silence. In one marriage Al and I counseled, the husband was so overbearing that his wife developed a response of talking like a child—the tone of her voice totally changed in conversations with him. He used his anger and put-downs to manipulate his wife into "submission." His continual criticism of even small household chores eroded her confidence. More commonly and less to the extreme, I've heard women say that their husbands made them feel like children by reminding them over and over to make a phone call or pay a bill.

Wives, we probably tempt our husbands to treat us this way by not following up with commitments or assignments. We should certainly take seriously our need to be responsible, and we should accept our husbands' constructive help in growing in these areas (if they are our weak areas). But we must remember that we are adults, not children, and we must communicate with our husbands in an adult way—even if we have "blown it" in some area.

Be an Adult and Speak the Truth

Growing up is hard to do! In many ways it doesn't get any easier just because we are adults. We may use the term "grown-up" for adult, but even we older women are still growing. Recently, I have grown in my conviction to love the truth. In several group settings it has been eye opening to observe dynamics and patterns between husbands and wives. Consciously and unconsciously we develop ways of silencing one another to avoid painful or embarrassing exposure of our weaknesses. One husband described the condition of the marriage relationship by saying, "We're doing good, aren't we?" The wife agreed, but later told the real truth when she knew she was in a "safe place" and would be heard. We certainly all need a safe environment where we can express our deepest hurts and fears, but we cannot afford to bypass the truth while waiting for the perfect atmosphere and tone.

Another wife began to express some ways her husband had hurt her, only to glance at him and immediately minimize what she had just said: "But you have changed a lot." It was obvious that she was fearful of his response—either in that setting or later when they would be alone.

In another situation the wife saw some patterns in their marriage clearly, but when she described them, her husband turned things back on her. He manipulated the situation in a way that left her thinking, "I must be crazy!"

By being silent, minimizing or agreeing outwardly while inwardly disagreeing, we are really being dishonest. We need to love the truth more than we even love the relationship with our husbands. We can apply Romans 1:25 powerfully to this type of situation.

> They exchanged the truth of God for a lie, and worshiped and served created things rather than the Creator.

Our love for the truth needs to motivate and propel us to speak the truth in love (Ephesians 4:15). If we are not honest, we do not give our husbands a chance to change and we do not give ourselves the chance to change. A dishonest answer "protects" both our husbands and ourselves from that which we need the most: healing, change and forgiveness. An honest answer sets the stage for God to do his work in our lives.

It is important to mention that some might fear their husbands' disapproval or anger. Others might fear an emotionally or even physically abusive response. If this is your situation, it will take much prayer and courage to be open and honest. Get advice from a spiritual woman or couple. Before talking to your husband, let him know that you have gotten advice and others know what you are sharing with him. Hopefully knowing this will help him to be more self-controlled since he will realize that others will also be aware of his response. It might even be best to communicate initially in the presence of a couple who can counsel your marriage dynamic. And always look to God's word for encouragement, comfort and strength (Psalm 34 would be a great focus scripture).

Speak the Truth in Love

Wives who have stuffed their feelings and hidden the truth need to have the courage to get the facts of their marriages out in the open. Recently I heard of a woman who said, "I want to mean what I say and say what I mean…and not be mean!" That's the spirit we should go for.

Certainly, as we are in the beginning stages of learning to speak the truth, we may be a bit raw in our presentation. Fear sometimes causes us to have emotion that is eruptive. But for too long, many of us have discipled the eruptive, emotional wife without trying to hear what she is really saying and feeling. Then the seemingly emotionally-controlled husband gets "off the hook" and doesn't get the discipling he so desperately needs.

If we want healthy marriages, we cannot control our emotions by stuffing our feelings. Thankfully, disciples will be patient with us to help us speak in love—that should always be our goal. And we will discover that the more we decide to be painfully honest, the more in control we will be emotionally. What we will be experiencing is the self-control that comes as a fruit of the Spirit, who works in our lives as we speak the truth (Galatians 5:22-23). Most of all, we need to not be afraid of the truth and to remember that "the truth will set [us] free" (John 8:32).

Accept Personal Responsibility

Being an adult has much to do with accepting responsibility. In most of the appointments that Al and I have with married couples, we help each person see and accept responsibility for his or her actions. Somehow, as human beings, we want to shift the blame: "If he wouldn't..., I wouldn't ..." Certainly, we are connected and we do affect each other tremendously. On the other hand, it is vital to recognize that I am the only one whom I can control and change. I don't know about you, but that's a big enough job for me!

Al and I had a recent exchange that showed me I still have some growing to do in this area of taking personal responsibility. We were getting ready to go on a date. Al was on the phone and I needed to know when we were going to leave. We have agreed not to interrupt each other when one of us is on the phone. All I wanted was a quick hand signal from Al, but what I got was a frown as he mouthed, "I'm on the phone!" I retreated, feeling aggravated and hurt.

As soon as he got off the phone, he came in and apologized and reminded me of our agreement. That should have taken care of it all, but I held on to my feelings. I let Al's response control my mood rather than (1) maturely accepting my responsibility for breaking our agreement and (2) forgiving Al for his response. Fortunately, I came to my senses and repented before I spoiled the whole evening. As I looked at my reaction, I realized that too often I connect to someone else's action when I should disconnect and be responsible for my own action.

You Are on His Team

God planned for the wife to be a helper "suitable" for the husband. It was God's intent for husband and wife to be together—we need each other. We make a great team...that is, when we work with each other rather than against each other. Couples are often quite different. One husband tells about seeing their differences clearly when they were on their honeymoon. They went mountain climbing—he was determined to get to the top no matter what; she wanted to have fun along the way. If it had been up to the wife, they never would have reached the top. If it had been up to the husband, they would have had no fun. As a team they were able to have fun reaching the top.

In our marriages, most of us have different strengths and weaknesses. It is amazing to see the incredible way God works to blend us together to be a team. We also feel the destructive pulls from Satan to use our differences to divide us. It is up to us individually to appreciate each other and to determine to do our part to work together. The Proverbs 31 wife is a great example of being a suitable helper:

> Her husband has full confidence in her
>   and lacks nothing of value.
> (Proverbs 31:11)

Part of the beauty of marriage is seeing how much better and more effective we are as a team than by ourselves. And our team is one of two adults, being honest with each other and with those in our lives. Forging that kind of team is scary at times, but with God's help we can push through our fear and bring glory to him through our marriages.

INTO YOUR HEART

being critical. Need to ~~properly~~ [?] elaborate mercy

1. In what ways have you mothered your husband?

2. How have you seen yourself as the child?

3. Can you see areas in your marriage in which you need to be more honest? Be courageous enough to share them with your husband. Pray and ask for advice if you are fearful.

4. Are there areas in your marriage that you and your husband have not been honest with others about? Are you willing to be honest and get help in these areas? Is truth more important to you than "keeping the peace" with your husband?

5. What are some ways that you and your husband work together well as a team, balancing each other's strengths and weaknesses?

6. Write any other response to this chapter and commitments you want to make.

5. The way he thinks + plans ahead + I get things done + vice versa, when I forget, Collin remembers + vice versa.

Being honest is more important than keeping the peace.

3/28/03 Speaking the truth in love.
→ I feel that Collin can be more
honest w/ me; by being more
vulnerable, open + communicates
the things he sees. He says or
opens up only when I ask;
+ his answers reveal that he
is not happy w/ the situation
(whatever is discussed). I
feel hurt; why did he not say
something b4. It makes me
feel that we are not on the same
sheet of music because if I
don't ask, it would not be said.
What if I don't ask?

I guess I need to trust
God, that he will reveal things
in its/his own time. God is in
control. Commit this to prayer.
Pray that God would put things in
my ♥ that needs addressing + he

7/14/06
This was sed. He voluntering
opens up.

54

will provide the time & atmosphere, (w/ my help) for Collin to express how he feels + to soften my ♡ to accept his views + see the truth + the ♡ to △.

★ Ask myself, does Collin feel that if he expresses himself (the truth) would it make a difference.

I think that he would feel that it would not make a difference. That I would do what Gunell wants to do. God, a I apologise for the things I have done to make Collin feel this way. Help me to listen to him carefully + at the end ask myself + him how can I △, or in what ways does he want me to △

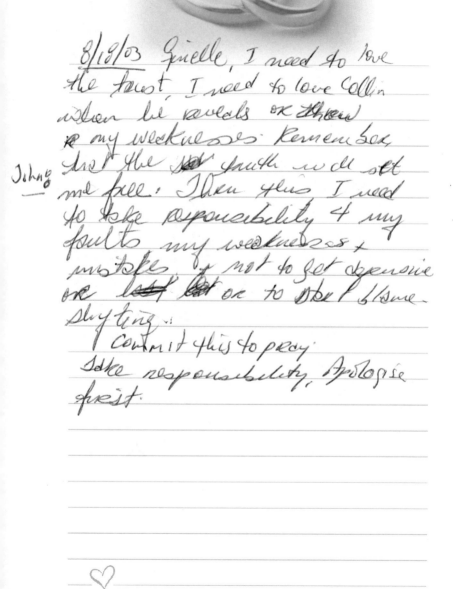

8/19/03 Ginelle, I need to love
the Trust. I need to love Collin
when he reveals or threw
is my weaknesses. Remember
that the truth will set
me free. Then this I need
to take responsibility 4 my
faults my weaknesses +
mistakes, + not to get defensive
or lash out or to start blame
shifting.
Commit this to pray.
Take responsibility. Apologise
first.

Johny

♡

Effective Communication

Handwritten notes:

- Disrespect shown thru looks & tone of voice
- * Understand how each one thinks

Eph 4:29 — The golden rule of effective communication —
P 70

♡ GEB

> Marriage can be <u>no more satisfying or happy than the degree</u>
> <u>to which you open your heart and mind with your spouse</u>....
> How can we be friends if we do not talk, and how can we be
> lovers if we are not friends?[1]

Handwritten note: OK That's cleared up.

Communication is challenging, pure and simple. Communication between a man and a woman is doubly challenging! In fact, communication is the number one problem in most marriages. I have heard the following statistic: a woman has the capacity for using 50,000 words a day while a man has the capacity for using 25,000. Upon hearing this, some women might say, "I think my husband uses up 24,950 of his words before he comes home from work. Then I get the other fifty!" And if these same women are at home with young children, their husbands might say, "My wife uses up fifty of hers with the kids during the day, and I get the other 49,950 when I get home!"

We laugh at this scenario because in many marriages the wife is more verbal than the husband. We have to realize, though, that sometimes the husband is more verbal. So, one way or the other, each partner generally differs from the other in communication skills. Then add in the different backgrounds, experiences, perceptions and ideals that the two people bring into the relationship. It is easy to see why communication is a challenge.

Real communication occurs when what is said is heard the way it was intended. The message that is sent is the same message that is received. It is helpful to "play back" and respond to verify the message that was sent. It may seem cumbersome to say, "I hear you saying.... Is that what you meant?" But this process helps to clarify before we respond or even react.

Before marriage, we dream of finding that "soul mate," the one to whom we can pour out our hearts and share our inmost thoughts. When Al and I dated, we seemed to be able to talk about anything—the communication flowed. Sometimes, though, in the midst of babies, work, ministry and life in general, that "flow" got blocked. Communication takes work, and after thirty-nine years of marriage, we are still working on it. We have learned a lot, but we have found that it is a lifelong process.

Verbal and Nonverbal Communication

There are two modes of communication: verbal and nonverbal. Our tones, sighs, body language and even our silence speak volumes about what is on our hearts. All these things considered, it is understandable that there are many opportunities for miscommunication.

Verbal

When we talk, it is a challenge to accurately connect with our words. For example, consider the following exchange between a husband and wife:

> He says, "You spent $150 for groceries this week?"
> She says, "Why do you always think I spend too much for groceries?"
> He says, "I was just amazed they cost that much and wondered why it was more than usual. Why are you getting defensive?"
> She says, "You always accuse me of spending too much money. Why don't you just go buy groceries yourself so you can see how much they cost."
> He says, "I just asked a simple question. I was not accusing you of anything."
> She says, "Well, that's what I heard."
> He says, "Well, you didn't hear what I meant."

He said something that she didn't hear, and she heard something that he didn't say.

Nonverbal

Though more subtle and less direct, our nonverbal communication is vitally important to examine. Our tone of voice is a big factor. A strong angry tone will probably cause our husbands to shut down or react. Proverbs 15:1 states that

> *A gentle answer turns away wrath,*
> *but a harsh word stirs up anger.*

Even with right words a woman's tone of voice can communicate disapproval. This can wound her husband and tempt him to be defensive. Inappropriate timing for a laugh can hurt a husband's feelings and cause him to feel that you are making fun of him. I still remember one of our girls as a toddler in response to our laughter, crying and saying, "Not bery funny!" Some adults have similar feelings, but may not express the hurt as clearly as a child would.

At times I communicate resistance and hesitancy to Al with nothing more than a wordless sigh.

Husbands have told me that their wives show disrespect to them through their looks and tone of voice. Wives, we know what they are talking about! Body language is revealing. When we meet with a couple, we can tell a lot about the condition of their relationship before any words are spoken. If they are sitting far apart or one of them has his or her arms folded tightly, we can guess they are not communicating very well.

A warning sign to Al in our communication is my silence. Of course, there is a good and comfortable type of silence, but I'm talking about the "cold wall" of silence that blocks out others...especially our husbands. Even when we have a pleasant expression on our faces, it is alarming how loudly that "silence" screams, "I am upset with you. I am not willing to talk about it. Leave me alone!"

What a Difference Our Differences Make

One of the most vital principles is understanding how each other thinks. Invariably each of us is inclined to expect the other to think and respond as we would. Herein lies the problem! Men and women are generally very different in their thinking and communication. Early in our marriage Al and I became well aware of some of these differences as we "bumped" from time to time trying to understand each other. It was not until a few years ago that we realized that many of our differences were not just our own quirks, but were typical of most men and women. A book that conveyed this to us in a clever and informative way was John Gray's *Men Are from Mars, Women Are from Venus.* Kay refers to this book in chapter 2 as she reminds us that we are actually from the same planet and do have the same basic needs in life. This being true, Gray does show us some of the ways we are different in our communication styles.

Offering Unsolicited Help

Al read some of Gray's book before I did, and then I had a somewhat painful introduction to the principles he had been reading about. He was putting Christmas boxes back on the shelves in the garage. I went out to help him and offered a few very helpful suggestions as to how he could do it. He said, "Gloria, I will put these boxes away, and you need to go read that book!"

I left the job with him, but I felt aggravated and totally confused because I was only trying to help. After reading the book, I saw that my offering unsolicited help to Al communicated to him that I did not trust him to do the job correctly. Prior to that I would have thought he was just in a bad mood or that I had done something wrong earlier. That line of thinking escalates the interaction and introduces lots of unnecessary baggage.

Nothing undermines a man's confidence like his wife's corrections and criticisms. How often do you comment on your husband's driving technique or tell him how to do something? It is harmful enough if you do it in private, but it communicates immense disrespect if done in front of the children or others.

Problem-Solving

Men are problem-solvers by nature. They deal with problems by thinking silently, preferably in their "cave" as Gray describes it. Men tend to handle this problem-solving stress by watching TV, jogging or playing sports. Women, on the other hand, tend to solve problems by thinking aloud and talking through every aspect, big or small. The more we talk, the better we feel, and eventually we see things more clearly. Complications arise when the wife brings up something as it comes to her mind—if it has a negative, "problem" sound, the problem-solving husband immediately feels responsible for the solution whether that was asked for by the wife or not. A typical exchange might go like this:

> Tom (on the spur of the moment): Let's have the neighbors over for dinner.
> Joan: I'm not sure this is a good time.
> Tom: There never seems to be a good time for you. It won't be any trouble; I'll grill hamburgers.
> Joan: (sighs and rolls her eyes)

Tom is aggravated with Joan. He feels that Joan is usually resistant to his suggestions and makes too much out of something simple. Joan feels that Tom is totally insensitive to all that is involved in preparing a meal, and she feels misjudged about her desire to be hospitable.

A helpful hint for this situation: the wife should make a positive statement first and then add her concerns. For example, "That's a great idea, and it would be nice to have them over. Could I tell you some of the things that I think we need to consider before we do that?"

If you want your husband to hear what you are feeling or to simply discuss some issue, it helps to let him know what you want. You might ask, "Is this a good time for us to talk? I would like to tell you some of my thoughts and feelings about…" That prepares him to listen rather than to go into his problem-solving mode.

Asking Questions

Another aspect of our communication that needed to change was the way I ask questions. For example, I used to ask Al, "What time is the meeting?" Then I would be totally confused by his sometimes-irritated response. I learned to ask, "Do you know what time the meeting is?" My first question made Al feel that I expected him to have the answer. The second approach did not make him feel defensive. Sometimes rather simple adjustments on our part can make the difference between a good interaction and a fight.

Hinting

Another way of communicating I have had to change is my hinting. For example, I might mention to Al that the trash can is full, meaning that I would like him to empty it. He would much prefer that I just make a direct request as opposed to beating around the bush.

I have also learned that it seems to make a difference if I say, "Would/will you?" versus "Could/can you?" I still do not fully understand that, but Al says for him it is true! As wives, we might find that when we ask, "Could you take out the trash?" our husbands might be tempted to say, "Yes, I could take it out. Do you want me to take it out?" So, be direct and don't try to soften a request by hinting at it.

You need to find out for sure how to communicate most clearly with your own husband. Ask him if there are better ways for you to ask questions or state requests. Then listen and be humble enough to communicate in the very best way for him.

Talking to Yourself

We think much faster than we speak. Have you ever been aware of the multiple and varied thoughts going through your mind at the same time you are in a conversation with someone? One of the "channels" in which we often think is a very destructive one. It is negative "self talk" fueled by the lies and half-truths of Satan. Some of the things we say to ourselves are "I'll never change," "Someone else could do this much better than I can," "I can't," "My thinking is so off-base." This negative type of thinking definitely affects our conversations with other people, even though these specific thoughts are usually kept in our own minds and not said aloud. One of the scriptures that helps me in this area is 2 Corinthians 10:5: "...and we take captive every thought to make it obedient to Christ."

In our marriage dynamics we may have these conversations with ourselves—arguing back and forth—without ever saying a word to our husbands! I still remember one such conversation with myself several years ago: When Al came home from work, he seemed edgy. Without saying anything to him, I immediately started my self talk about how unfair it was for him to still be upset about our not making love that morning…he hadn't even let me know he wanted to…and we woke up too late anyway…and on and on!

When I finally asked him if he was upset with me, he assured me he wasn't. He said his project at work had not gone well that day. I wish I could say that was the only time I ever thought like that and came to wrong conclusions, but it is not. We do not want someone else to assume what we think and feel, so we need to stop trying to read our husbands' minds as well. (See Matthew 7:12.)

Listening to Our Husbands

It is very important to learn to focus and devote full attention to our husbands when they are talking with us. Learning to be a good listener is vital to our communication skills.

> *Everyone should be quick to listen, slow to speak and slow to become angry. (James 1:19)*

One way to work on our listening skills is to try to restate what the other person said to us (as mentioned earlier). Too often we are thinking of an answer or rebuttal to what has just been said. Statements such as "Let me see if I heard you correctly" and "Is this what you wanted me to hear?" are good tools to hone our listening skills. If we are "quick to listen" to what someone says, it will be evident, and it communicates a genuine interest in that person.

Spiritual Communication

Nothing is more essential to deep communication in marriage than our relationship with God. In Solomon's often quoted statement, "Two are better than one...," he ends the passage with, "A cord of three strands is not quickly broken" (Ecclesiastes 4:9-12). The most powerful "third strand" is God. From the beginning of our marriage, Al and I have prayed together daily. We weren't really told to do that; it just seemed like the thing to do. We needed to actively involve God in our daily lives. Without realizing it at the time, we were drawing on the strength that we now refer to as the "spiritual glue of our marriage." We describe our prayer time as saying "good morning" and "good night" to God together.

I know of no other specific input that we have given other couples more consistently or with more conviction than to pray together daily. You can certainly initiate the prayer time, especially if your husband has indicated that it would help him. It is important, however, not to resort to nagging or having a self-righteous attitude.

In addition to our daily praying, Al and I treasure "prayer walk" times that are longer and more concentrated. This is a highlight of our special get-away times, overnighters and anniversary celebrations. These times bond us more deeply as we share our hearts and concerns. I cannot imagine how difficult even day-to-day communication would be without a common foundation in our love for God and his word.

I have shared with you some of the specific things that have helped Al and me grow in our relationship. My charge to you is to strive to keep growing in your communication with your husband. Look for your patterns and resolve to help each other communicate more effectively. It helps if you take responsibility for what your husband hears you say—whether verbally or nonverbally. You can do something about your part. Be thankful for discipling and commit (with your husband) to be open with the couple discipling you; they can help you in your communication with each other.

Finally, I encourage you to memorize what Al and I call the "golden rule of communication":

> *Do not let any unwholesome talk come out of your mouths, but only what is helpful for building others up according to their needs, that it may benefit those who listen. (Ephesians 4:29)*

If you put that into practice, you will not only improve your marriage, but you will be training your children to have more effective communication skills as well.

We serve a communicating God, and he will help us communicate more clearly and more lovingly as we continue to learn from him.

NOTES

1. Sam and Geri Laing, *Friends and Lovers* (Billerica, Mass.: Discipleship Publications International, 1996), 29.

INTO YOUR HEART

1. Do you know specific ways that you communicate disrespect to your husband? If so, list them and pray about catching yourself before you do them. If not, ask your husband, and listen attentively and nondefensively to his answer.

2. What part does silence play in your communication? In what ways is it good? In what ways is it bad?

3. Think of some men-women differences that affect your communication with your husband. Write them down so you can be aware of what your challenges are and so you can go about overcoming them.

4. Identify some of the negative "self talk" that you do. Share it with someone who can help you.

5. How often are you praying with your husband? What can you do that will encourage this to happen more often in your relationship?

6. Write any other response to this chapter and commitments you want to make.

Talk about
• Communication + listening to Collin
  not remembering; not clear (Michelle + Bee)
• Devo times
• Intimacy - not breathing.

3/30/03 Differences
- Offering unsolicited help - shows
I do not trust Collin. Criticisms +
correction undermines Collin's
confidence
- Problem-solving - Men's nature
is to solve the problem of the
solution
+ 1st make a positive statement, then
add my concerns. p65
- Ask questions differently.
- Hinting - Do not hint, simply
directly request things. The trash
can is full vs would take
the out the trash.
- Ask him if there is a way he
prefers me to ask questions or
requests
- No self talking which is negative
talk + Do not assume what Collin
is thinking. Simply. Ask.

72

• Be a good listener to Collin. Give
him my full attention when he
speaks. I need to grow tremendously
in this area. Collin's words are
"Nobody listens to me."
Ask is this what you mean...
" is this what you wanted me to hear.
• Pray together. The third strand is God.
Pull on it when praying together.

8/19/03

Speak clearly. eg. Asking Michelle
to move the car 4 the BBQ. I did did
not b/c she was having a BBQ the week
b4. Collin got the impression
that I had specifically ask
her to move the car.

I need to work on effective
communication w/ Collin. Think
about what I am saying.

♡

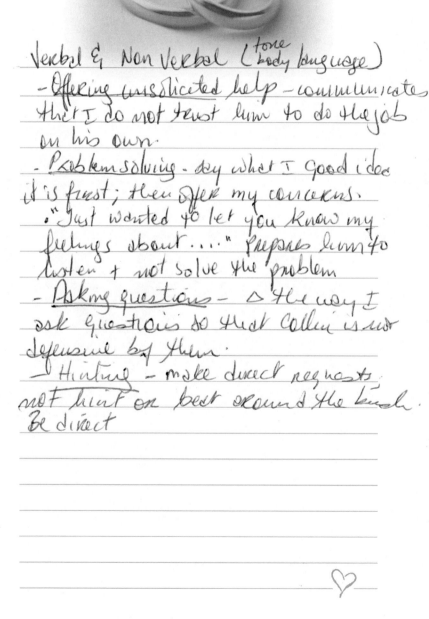

Verbal & Non Verbal (tone body language)
- Offering unsolicited help - communicate
that I do not trust him to do the job
on his own.
- Problem solving. Say what I good idea
it is first; then offer my concerns.
."Just wanted to let you know my
feelings about...." Prepares him to
listen + not solve the problem
- Asking questions - Δ the way I
ask questions so that Collin is not
defensive by them.
- Hinting - make direct requests.
not hint or beat around the bush.
Be direct

Hitting the Bumps

5

KSM

> Reckless words pierce like a sword,
>   but the tongue of the wise brings healing.
> > > Proverbs 12:18

We call them "bumps" but they feel more like cataclysmic earthquakes of Biblical proportion. They leave us raw, wounded, helpless and torn. We can speak lightly about them the day after, but in the middle of the night we are tearful and angry. These bumps are disagreements, arguments, fights, conflicts between husband and wife.

During my dating relationship and engagement to Randy, we rarely quarreled. There were times we hurt each other's feelings or let each other down, but we seldom exchanged "words" or became angry with each other. In fact, we used to say we would never argue. Our theory was that if two people were close to God, then they would be able to be close to each other at all times and never be in conflict. I am sure that when we espoused that philosophy many of our married friends chuckled, and said to themselves, "Just wait." But we were sure of ourselves and felt that our love was higher and deeper and better than anyone else could understand. We marched down the aisle with confidence and hope, certain that nothing would injure our love for each other.

I do not even remember our first argument. It was probably several little disagreements at first. But when we finally realized that yes, we love each other and yes, we do have arguments, it was a bit of a shock! My naiveté quickly diminished when I understood that any two human beings would not always be on the same wavelength. We learned that we had different needs, backgrounds and perspectives that would put us at odds with each other. Surprise! Randy and I both had very strong opinions about very many things, and neither of us was willing to easily let go of those opinions!

Any two people who have been married for any length of time have figured out what they generally fight about. It may be money, household responsibilities, the kids, the in-laws or sex. For me, I wanted Randy to be a "fix-it" person. If difficulties or challenges came up, I went to him for solutions. If he did not have the solution I wanted, I was disappointed in him. Conflict would erupt if he did not say or do exactly the right thing and take the problem away, or at least get right on it. I believe one of our biggest battles was the time he told me to "be a woman" and take care of a problem myself! Where was my knight in shining armor? Where was my hero, my superman, my protector? The truth is, Randy does take care of me in countless ways. But there are only so many things that a husband can do—and some things he simply cannot do for his wife, regardless of how wonderful he is. I am so thankful for the great husband that he is to me, but I still have to watch my attitude when he does not make the challenges of life just go away.

It is important to recognize the attitudes, thoughts and perspectives that lead you to conflict with your husband. These are the "buttons" that cause arguments and hurt feelings, and they can be avoided (or at least dealt with in a sensitive way). We do not have to keep arguing about the same things! We can learn how to approach hot topics without a dispute breaking out. We can live in peace with each other.

The Scriptures deal so often with the proper and godly way to have relationships with one another. There is no closer relationship than that of husband and wife, and yet so often couples ignore these Biblical guidelines in their marriages. God is clear about how to treat one another: "Honor one another above yourselves....Share with God's people who are in need....Do not repay anyone evil for evil....If it is possible, as far as it depends on you, live at peace with everyone" (Romans 12:10-18). "'In your anger do not sin': Do not let the sun go down while you are still angry, and do not give the devil a foothold....Get rid of all bitterness....Be kind and compassionate to one another, forgiving each other, just as in Christ God forgave you" (Ephesians 4:26-27, 31-32). "Therefore, as God's chosen people...clothe yourselves with compassion, kindness, humility, gentleness and patience" (Colossians 3:12). "Love is patient, love is kind. It does not envy, it does not boast, it is not proud. It is not rude, it is not self-seeking, it is not easily angered, it keeps no record of wrongs" (1 Corinthians 13:4-5). These words form the foundation of a solid marriage relationship and enable us to have the character that is needed when disagreements do arise. When we know that we are committed to love, gentleness and forgiveness, then even tense topics can be dealt with in a way that leads to unity.

In my own marriage and in counseling with numerous other couples, I have found that these scriptures, along with some basic common sense guidelines, can lead to a happy and close relationship between husband and wife.

Expect

As I have already mentioned, it is normal and natural to have conflict—disagreements will arise between you and your husband. If you do not expect this to happen, it will catch you off guard, your feelings will be hurt, and you'll be left questioning, "What just happened here?"

None of us looks forward to conflicts, but we need to be prepared for them when they do come. In the same way, it is crucial to expect resolution! In the midst of an argument, keep remembering that eventually you will make up. Sometimes in the middle of heated words it is hard to imagine that eventually you will be feeling loving and close. But you will! It is a sign of maturity in a relationship when you recognize that fact, even as you are struggling through the conflict. If you can see the light at the end of the tunnel, the tunnel is not quite so dark. Sometimes disagreements can be so intense that you cannot even fathom what the solution will be. This is when you must take heart and know that even if you cannot figure it out, God does have a solution. It may take a while to find it, but it is there. With help, prayer and perhaps guidance from good friends, you will be able to come together again and repair the damage that has been done. Expect resolution!

Sometimes we can even lighten a heavy situation by keeping our sense of humor—we need to remind each other that eventually we will be laughing about this disagreement. We can remind ourselves of our own weaknesses and quirks that have led to this conflict. But be careful about this. If you take lightly an issue that is very serious to your spouse, it may only intensify the situation. It is important to be sensitive to your husband and know when the problem is not something to joke about.

Accept

The definition of insanity is doing the same thing over and over again and expecting different results. There are some insane wives (and husbands) out there! We know that our husbands have certain likes and dislikes, particular moods and perspectives, or harmless habits that have been there for a lifetime. Yet we wives think that if we keep nagging, asking, wanting, fussing or whatever else we do, then they will change! This insanity on our part leads to incredible conflict. There are things that we must learn to accept. We need to stop trying to change our husbands into the image of what we want. Can you accept that your husband is a human being with frailties and that he will make mistakes? Can you overlook, in a spirit of graciousness, things that may be your pet peeves? For example, does your husband put ketchup on the nice omelet you just made? Does he hit the snooze button several times? Does he hog the remote? Does he...?

Remind yourself that these and many other little things are part of his makeup, part of what makes him who he is. Smile...and show grace just as you want him to show grace to you.

Christian women have a high standard for the men they marry, and rightfully so. But too often, our standards are so high that we frustrate our husbands and ourselves. Until we respect the fact that we cannot change our husbands, we will continually be facing conflicts. Only God can change another person's behavior, and even then only if that person is willing and wanting to change. Under the guise of helping our husbands to become more like Christ, we can in actuality want them to change to become more like us. While it is good and right to express our concerns and make our husbands aware of our own likes and dislikes, we must ultimately give them the freedom to be human beings.

Protect

While arguments and disagreements are sure to come, we can set boundaries to protect our relationships:

- Make a decision that you will not say or do things that are hurtful or dangerous.
- No matter how heated things may become, the "D" word (divorce) is never an option.
- Avoid using phrases like "You never" or "You always."

After being married a while, we know which issues are incredibly painful for our spouses, and we must resolve never to "hit below the belt"—bringing up past hurts or disappointments that will only serve to fuel the fire of an argument instead of being solution oriented. While an argument is going on, it is easy to become a bit irrational, but even then anyone can decide to refrain from statements that could injure beyond repair.

It is important to remember that you and your spouse are not the only ones who are affected by an argument. If you have children in the home, they are often painfully aware of problems between Mom and Dad. The best scenario is to protect them from any displays of tension between their parents, but that is sometimes impossible to do: they live with us, they know and see us, and they are very perceptive. One couple recently told us how their young son came into the room when they were in the midst of a conflict. The little three-year-old looked at his tearful mom and then declared with great authority to both of them: "You are best friends, you are married, you love each other." With that being said, he left the room, trusting that his parents would believe him and act accordingly.

If our children do see us having an argument with our husbands, it is also imperative that they see us make up. We should verbally express to them that Mom and Dad had a disagreement, but that they love each other and have said, "I am sorry." Children generally are not too upset about conflict unless it is unresolved conflict.

The challenge with addressing marital conflict is that each couple is so different, and each marriage is so unique. What is "joking" to some is "cutting" to others. For example, some men are very sensitive to the issue of aging, while others can laugh at their bald spots. Some are self-conscious about their weight, while others can talk openly about their expanding bellies. Each wife must be sensitive to her own husband and not expect him to respond as others might.

While the keys and guidelines suggested in this chapter are generally applicable to any couple, it is very important to get specific help regarding your own particular challenges. Some couples need much guidance in working out their difficulties, while other couples may just need a few reminders from time to time. It is such a blessing to be in God's church, where we have brothers and sisters who want to help us have marriages that bring glory to God. I personally am extremely grateful for the couples who have given helpful advice to Randy and me through the years. Any married people who say that they do not need help are usually the ones who need help the most. Do not be hesitant to ask for advice and counsel. In this way, you can have a marriage that is happy, fulfilled and peaceful. This is what God wants; it is what your husband wants; it is what you want.

Above all, my greatest recommendation in dealing with marriage bumps is to be a woman of prayer. Stay close to God and keep praying about the things that hurt you or concern you. Make a decision that you will not approach your husband about a problem before you have first approached God. Pray for wisdom, gentleness and self-control! Pray for forgiveness for yourself and the ability to forgive your husband. Above all, pray for love, which will bind you together with your husband in perfect unity (Colossians 3:14).

INTO YOUR HEART

1. When you and your husband hit a relational bump on your road to marital bliss, what type of bump does it tend to be:

   • a slight protrusion

   • a transmission-jarring roll of swollen asphalt

   • an ascending slope with a ten-foot drop on the other side

   In other words, how severe are the bumps you have? If they are severe, are you getting help from someone to deal with recurring patterns?

2. Do you quickly work through your conflicts, or do you allow them to affect you for hours, days, weeks or longer? *Collin is great w/ not letting it affect us for a longer time. He is quick to forgive & move on.*

3. What sins are usually involved on your part when you *my selfishness when CB does not respond the way I expect him to* and your husband have a conflict? Do you typically repent as soon as you see your sin? How willing are you to pray with your husband when you are in the middle of the conflict? *Need to pray more w/ CB*

4. Look again at the scriptures on pages 79-80. Which statement do you most need to take to heart as you work through conflicts in your marriage? *Col 3:12*

5. What boundaries do you place on yourself while in the midst of a difficult interchange with your husband? (See the suggestions on page 83.)

6. When you and your husband cannot seem to see eye to eye on a certain topic or situation, what hope is yours as a daughter of God?

7. Write any other response to this chapter and commitments you want to make.

Find encouraging things I like about CB & let him know about it daily. That will help w/ my attitude to be grateful, thus eager to resolve conflict. Go to God, rely on the scriptures

8/25-26/03
- Expect arguments; expect them
  to be resolve
- Accept. There R things that I
  need to learn to accept.
- Protect. Have ground rules during
  arguments. No Divorce word.
  no always - never, don't be
  hurtful!
- Pray

On Saturday, Aug 23 by Damita's
wedding, Collin + I had a dew
on being difficult times in
our lives together. We shared +
it was so amazing at the depth
of our sharing. We communicated.
I love it when I see Collin's
♡ open + exposed - I am seeing
it more + more.

♡

- I admire CB's openness + vulnerability
- He is such a good listener. This strength is being strengthened. He is growing in his strength
- He loves being on a team; he loves fellowship. He is a great friend. He is great @ keeping in touch w/ long distant friends

Col 3:12, 1 COR 13:4-5,
Eph 4:26-27. 31-32, Rom 12:10-18
Eph 4:29.

♡

Attitude Is 6
Everything

GEB

"If Momma ain't happy, ain't nobody happy!"

Women, we have power—power to determine the atmosphere and tone of our homes. God has given us that power, and he wants us to use it in a righteous way. Is your home warm and full of love? Or is your home cold and full of tension? Whether you like it or not, you are the determining factor. Your house might be a decorator's showpiece, but is it a place where your family and others feel welcomed and loved?

Making a house into a home encompasses so much more than interior decorating skills. Solomon acknowledges the woman's responsibility in Proverbs 14:1:

The wise woman builds her house,
*   but with her own hands the foolish*
*   one tears hers down.*

Al and I saw the truth of this proverb in the lives of a couple we knew several years ago. The wife transformed her military housing into a model home with her designing skills, but she brought crushing blows to her marriage with her unfaithfulness.

Your home is a reflection of you. It is your God-given privilege and responsibility to build your home to bring glory to God. Your attitude—where your heart is—defines the atmosphere of your home. What is your attitude about life? Do you have the "half full" or the "half empty" perspective? You may plod through your day-to-day routine feeling burdened and disappointed by life. On the other hand, you may see life as an adventure, not knowing what to expect, but knowing it won't be boring. Whatever your perspective is, it will certainly affect your own happiness level as well as the happiness level of those around you. God has given us his accurate perspective to shape our attitudes about life:

> *His divine power has given us everything we need*
> *for life and godliness through our knowledge of him*
> *who called us by his own glory and goodness.*
> *(2 Peter 1:3)*

God has not shortchanged us. He has given us everything we need to live a godly, content life. We can decide whether we will call on the power he has given us. Whatever our life situation, our attitude is our own individual choice.

For some of us a positive outlook comes more easily. Others may be more naturally inclined to have a critical, negative perspective. As disciples we are called to a high standard; we need to choose to have the attitude of Jesus. As women, we especially need to focus on three attitudes of Jesus: gratitude, contentment and joy. If we choose these attitudes, we can freshen and rejuvenate the atmosphere of our homes.

Attitude of Gratitude

Gratitude is not an optional attitude for God's people; we are commanded to be thankful:

> And whatever you do, whether in word or deed, do it all in the name of the Lord Jesus, giving thanks to God the Father through him. (Colossians 3:17)

> Give thanks in all circumstances, for this is God's will for you in Christ Jesus. (1 Thessalonians 5:18)

The command to be thankful is one of the most ignored exhortations in the Bible. Unfortunately, women are often the worst offenders because we quickly spot the one thing that is done wrong and overlook the majority of things done right. That response promotes criticalness, not gratitude. How easy it is to focus on what we do not have rather than on what we do have.

I discovered in myself a pattern of negative thinking that I have labeled my "whirlpool syndrome." One negative thought seems to trigger another negative thought resulting in a very down mood. I remember the time Al needed a shirt that I had forgotten to put in the dryer. In my thoughts I berated myself saying *I'm a terrible wife—I can't even keep my husband's clothes clean.* Suddenly a thank-you note that I had not written came to my thoughts, resulting in my thinking *I'm not a good friend either!* On the heels of that thought came *I should have spent more time with the girls today— I'm certainly not much of a mother.* This thought was quickly followed by *How could God be pleased with me?* Satan is a master at proving that our negative thoughts are true. Notice the self-focus and the total absence of gratitude in this whirlpool of thoughts.

Now in most of my counseling appointments with other women I ask, "How thankful have you been?" The answer is generally, "I haven't been thankful." My direction is to make a "thankful list." This is the quickest way I know to turn worried, fearful, critical, negative thoughts into positive God-centered thoughts. It is all too common to take good things for granted and not even acknowledge them. When we focus on being thankful, our own hearts and attitudes change, thus affecting others for good.

Expressing thanks to God is of utmost importance, but we also need to model and teach gratitude to each other in the home. Basic good manners such as saying "Please" and "Thank you" need to be the common practice. I am grateful today for the example of my mom and dad, who established a thankful atmosphere in our home. One of the most vivid memories of my dad, who was living with us until his death at ninety years old, was his thanking us for everything we did for him, no matter how small. Needless to say, that made our caring for him much easier, but more than that, his attitude of gratitude was an incredible upward call to Al and me.

As wives we need to be sure to express appreciation to our husbands for the ways they care for us and our families. A genuine heartfelt "Thank you for the way you lead our family" would certainly encourage most husbands. Al says that the atmosphere of encouragement and appreciation communicated continually through words, looks and actions means much to a husband. Expressing gratitude specifically and frequently to your husband not only helps the atmosphere in your home, but also sets a great example for anyone around you. Gratitude is contagious.

Attitude of Contentment

Today's advertising is intended to breed discontentment. There is always something bigger, better, longer lasting, new and improved—anything to make us want more. At every turn we can see neighbors or family who have finer houses and newer cars. It is so tempting to compare what we have with the "more" that others have. That comparison usually leads to discontentment. In other words, it is challenging to have the attitude of contentment!

It helps to remember the way Paul met this challenge of remaining content:

> I am not saying this because I am in need, for I have learned to be content whatever the circumstances. I know what it is to be in need, and I know what it is to have plenty. I have learned the secret of being content in any and every situation, whether well fed or hungry, whether living in plenty or in want. I can do everything through him who gives me strength. (Philippians 4:11-13)

It is encouraging to know that Paul learned to be content. If Paul learned it, we can learn it as well. As with Paul, we will go through many different circumstances to teach us to rely on God's strength. What situation are you in at this moment? Are you content? You might be saying, "How can I possibly be content? The washer is broken, company is coming for dinner, and the baby is sick!" Know that God can teach you to be content whatever the circumstances.

As I think of discontent women I have counseled or times that I have been discontent, I see an underlying desire for control. It seems that as long as we are "in control" everything is okay, but as soon as something is out of our hands we are discontent. Can you identify with any of these thoughts:

"Why do we have to move again?"

"Why can't I have another baby?"

"I wish I didn't have to work."

"No one cares about my family."

"I wish I had time to relax."

"Why doesn't my husband pray with me?"

These thoughts must be honestly faced and worked through, but if we aren't on our guard, they can become the breeding ground for discontentment.

Contentment does not depend on perfect circumstances; rather, it depends on a decision to rely on God. Thankfully, that helps us in the midst of all kinds of situations. Each time we choose to rely on God, we learn that his way works, and we are content with God's will—God's control.

Having the attitude of contentment in marriage is much more than just a nice thought. Being content is essential in building a godly home. A discontent wife is a burden to her husband. (See Proverbs 21:9.) She communicates verbally and nonverbally that nothing is good enough and that she cannot be pleased. In some cases a wife's discontentment may be the cause of going into major debt or the incentive for her getting a job. Her desire for more and more may go beyond what her husband can provide. If *he* cannot provide the special extras, *she* will.

Husbands feel responsible for the happiness of their wives. A wife's discontentment is a reflection on a husband—he can feel like a failure. In contrast, a content wife is a great strength to her husband. Her reliance on God enables her to be a real helper, able to carry her part of the load. Together they can work to please God.

Decide to have the attitude of contentment. Contentment is not only godly; it is contagious.

Attitude of Joy

In a rerun of the TV show *All in the Family,* Archie Bunker stated, "I ain't against happiness in the house. I just don't want nobody to show it!" It seems that some people are more comfortable with negativism than with a positive approach to life. We may laugh at Archie Bunker, but a person who takes that stance toward life is not a pleasant companion.

Anyone can be happy under the right circumstances, but for the disciple, joy is possible and constant because it depends on what Christ has done. Joy is a fruit of the Spirit, available for all of us as followers of Christ. We often equate happiness with joy, then feel very confused during hard times. Even during the worst of times we can choose to have a joyful attitude because our attitudes are based on God's Spirit, not on circumstances nor our feelings. I am not talking about a superficial, fake "Pollyanna" attitude. True joy is experienced through a deep and faithful walk with God.

My own joy level has been challenged to the limit—losing three babies, experiencing the deaths of Al's mom and both of my parents as well as dealing with some of the most difficult situations in the church. On my own I would be in the depths of despair, but with God's word and power I can have hope, security and yes…joy. Habakkuk 3:17-18 is a continual encouragement to help me keep a joyful focus:

> *Though the fig tree does not bud*
> *   and there are no grapes on the vines,*
> *though the olive crop fails*
> *   and the fields produce no food,*
> *though there are no sheep in the pen*
> *   and no cattle in the stalls,*
> *yet I will rejoice in the Lord,*
> *   I will be joyful in God my Savior.*

Pouring my heart out to God and being open with Al and the people God has put in my life enables me to unload my burdens and to experience the joy from God's Spirit.

How can we as wives display joy in our homes? By being open and vulnerable yet faithful, using kind words, smiling often, complimenting others, having polite exchanges, expressing laughter as well as tears of joy and counting blessings.

Proverbs 15:13 says, "A happy heart makes the face cheerful" and Proverbs 15:30 says, "A cheerful look brings joy to the heart." Our faces say much about what is in our hearts. Smiles are contagious—joy is contagious.

God worked through Paul and his life's circumstances to challenge and convict our hearts about the attitudes of gratitude, contentment and joy in Philippians 4:4-7:

> Rejoice in the Lord always. I will say it again: Rejoice! Let your gentleness be evident to all. The Lord is near. Do not be anxious about anything, but in everything, by prayer and petition, with thanksgiving, present your requests to God. And the peace of God, which transcends all understanding, will guard your hearts and your minds in Christ Jesus.

It is obvious that these three attitudes are interrelated, and as I have stated, contagious. Wouldn't it be great to see an epidemic of gratitude, a spreading of contentment and an outbreak of joy in all our homes? If we fill our homes in this way, we will be a lot happier, and our homes will be beacons of light drawing other families to God's way.

There is no place where our own personal righteousness is tested more than in the home. We can easily let our guard down, and in doing so, give Satan a foothold. Decide to make a difference in your home as you put into practice the attitudes of Christ.

INTO YOUR HEART

1. Right now, how would you rate the atmosphere in your home with #1 being "tense and cold" and #10 being "happy and warm"? What can you do to have "better numbers" in this area?

2. Write out a "thankful list." When you are tempted to be ungrateful, go back and look at the list...and praise God for his blessings.

3. Do you ever deal with the "whirlpool syndrome" in your thinking (one negative self-thought after another)? How can being grateful help you to break free of the downward pull of the whirlpool?

4. How do you express appreciation to your husband through words, looks and actions?

5. Does your husband see you as content? To be sure, ask him.

6. What challenges your joy level? Which passage of Scripture is most helpful to you to restore your joy?

7. Write any other response to this chapter and commitments you want to make.

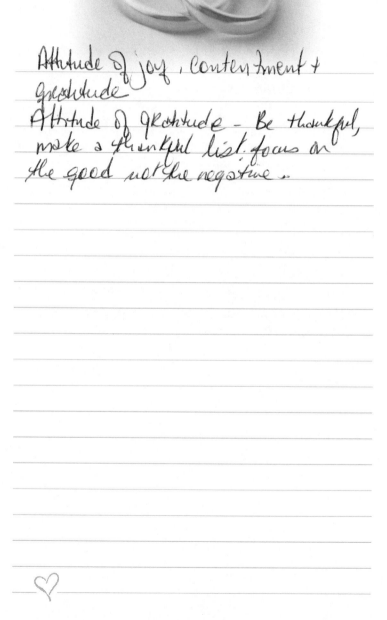

Attitude of joy, Contentment +
gratitude
Attitude of gratitude - Be thankful,
make a thankful list. focus on
the good not the negative.

♡

Intimacy
for Life

7

♡ *KSM*

Like an apple tree among the trees of the forest
    is my lover among the young men.
I delight to sit in his shade,
    and his fruit is sweet to my taste.
He has taken me to the banquet hall,
    and his banner over me is love.
Strengthen me with raisins,
    refresh me with apples,
    for I am faint with love.
His left arm is under my head,
    and his right arm embraces me.

                    Song of Solomon 2:3-6

May your fountain be blessed,
    and may you rejoice in the wife of your youth.
A loving doe, a graceful deer—
    may her breasts satisfy you always,
    may you ever be captivated by her love.

                    Proverbs 5:19

"For this reason a man will leave his father and moth-er and be united to his wife, and the two will become one flesh. This is a profound mystery...."

Ephesians 5:31-32

Whoever said that God is a prude? He is the cre-ator of our bodies and our sexual natures; he is the inventor of the sexual act. His plan is for sex to be a pleasurable experience between a husband and wife, and furthermore, for married couples to be satisfied always by each other. It is true that the sexual act is the means to procreation, but it is also true that God intended sex to be an enjoyable union, joining two human beings in an incomparable way. Two people becoming one...two people finding ecstasy in each other's arms...two people knowing each other com-pletely and intimately—this is God's doing! Sex is good, and God can work to make it even better as time goes by.

"Honeymoons are wasted on amateurs." I don't know who coined this phrase, but it does have a spark of truth to it. While we thoroughly enjoyed our honey-moon twenty-four years ago, Randy and I would have an even better time if we had a week at the same place today. Our intimacy has deepened; we know each other's likes and dislikes; we have figured out the best ways to bring each other pleasure and delight. The exciting thing is that we are still learning about each other, and enjoy-ing every minute of it! We have a lifetime in which to do this. I can look forward to each intimate time with antic-ipation because it can always be fresh and new.

The day before my wedding, I showed my father the ring I had picked out for Randy. I was so proud of that ring, knowing that it was the symbol of our love and life together. I remember my father pointing to the ring he wore on his finger and saying, "I hope it will last as long as this ring has lasted." Married almost thir-ty years, he was assuring me that the best was yet to come. Sadly, my dad died one year later, but the mem-ory of his comment is a constant reminder to me that intimacy is for life.

Better As the Years Go By

How sad that the world can trick us into thinking that the thrill is gone after a few years of marriage. On the contrary, the more time we have, the more oppor-tunity we have to make our relationship better and even more passionate. Our commitment to each other sees us through any difficulties that threaten our inti-macy. Yes, there are times in any marriage when things can get stale. Babies, job stress, illness, sadness—all of these life challenges can take the fire out of anyone's sex life. But if we don't give up on each other, and if we recognize that we have a lifetime to sort out the prob-lems, we will light the fires again. God's plan for the sexual relationship is fairly simple: a man and a woman committed to one another for life will be able to enjoy each other's bodies throughout their lives. But human beings have a tendency to complicate the simple things of life. Because of our backgrounds, misconceptions, traditions and sins, it is a challenge for some of us to accept and fully participate in the sexual act in the way God intended.

In some instances, people have serious physical challenges that hinder the sexual relationship. If this is your situation, I urge you to go beyond this book and get help so that you can be healed, either emotionally or physically. Be sure to read the next chapter on "Sexual Specifics" by Gloria and consider the list of helpful books at the end of this book. I also encourage you to get help from another person—preferably an older woman who is a disciple, or if necessary, from a professional counselor or doctor.

If your situation involves a chronic disease that affects your sexual relationship, learn ways to give to each other that work for you. Remember that intimacy involves more than passionate physical lovemaking. It also involves holding, touching, emotional closeness and contentment with each other.

Variety Is the Spice of Life

Some of us might be dealing with some other problems: boredom, laziness or inertia. We have simply given in to the "same-old, same-old" and just need a nudge to liven things up a bit. If this is where you are, hopefully this chapter will stimulate your thinking, and maybe a few other parts of you, so that you will wake up sexually. This part of your life and your marriage is incredibly important. Do not neglect it—make it all that God wants it to be.

Possibly the most obvious yet most quickly forgotten advice to married women is found in the adage "Variety is the spice of life." This statement is true in just about every aspect of our lives. For example, I love steak and potatoes. Give me a filet, cooked medium rare, a nice baked potato with salt and butter, and I am a happy woman. I like this meal, and I like it often. But give it to me tonight and tomorrow and the next day and the next, and surely I will tire of it. I will be longing for fresh green vegetables, a tuna sandwich, spaghetti or even peanut butter. No matter how good steak and potatoes are, I was not made to eat the exact same food day after day. I want to savor the flavors of a variety of foods.

The same principle applies to the sexual relationship. Some couples have a routine for their lovemaking that is satisfying to some degree, but certainly not very exciting. It fulfills all the requirements for sex, but is boring and lacks imagination. Some wives want to keep it that way, while their husbands long for more variety. A wife who is not willing to step out of her comfort zone to meet her husband's needs is forgetting the role that only she can play in helping her husband overcome sexual temptation. She is also forgetting that God made the sexual relationship to be pure and fun.

Other wives want to change the routine, but wait for their husbands to do it. Be proactive! Be creative! Discover what is exciting to both of you and then initiate it. This includes things like sexy new nightgowns, candles, different times and places for lovemaking, writing inviting notes to your husband—whatever it takes to make the time special for the two of you.

"The two of you" is really what it is all about. Some women have hindered their sexual relationship with their husbands by comparing themselves with others. They compare their bodies to those they see in the magazines or on television. They compare their bodies to how they looked thirty years ago. (As Gypsy Rose Lee said, "I have everything I had twenty years ago, only it's all a little bit lower.") We should strive to look our best for our husbands, but we should also be comfortable in our bodies, not self-conscious. Insecurity is not a sexy attitude for a wife to have.

Sometimes women compare their sexual habits to those of other married women, and then wonder if there is something wrong if they don't "measure up": *That couple makes love three times a week, and we only do it one time a week. Is something wrong with us?* They compare their husbands to other women's husbands: *Her husband always brings flowers home when he wants to make love. Why doesn't my husband do that?* This comparing is not right or healthy! My relationship with my husband is unique and incomparable. While I can and should learn from others, I must not make the mistake of thinking that what is pleasing and satisfying to another couple would be the same for us.

It is crucial that we know our own husbands' needs and desires so that we can fulfill them. Different men like different things. What does your husband like? What does he want? Does he like the sexy negligee, or does he prefer you *au naturel*? Does spontaneity make him happy, or would he prefer planning and thinking about being together throughout the day? Does he like you to wear perfume and makeup, or would those get in the way of his senses? Study your husband! Listen for cues and ask questions to learn how to be a better lover for him.

Growing Together

"People change and forget to tell each other" was writer Lillian Hellman's answer to why relationships go stale. We must never assume that what worked ten, twenty or thirty years ago is what will work today. The sexual act is fairly basic, but what leads up to it includes a variety of styles and preferences. Be willing to try new things. Be aware that your husband's tastes and his sex drive may change. Be aware that yours may change too! Do not hesitate to talk about your own needs and to let him know what you like. There may be times when pain or discomfort interferes with having intercourse. Be open to talking and arriving at solutions together.

In later years some women find that menopausal symptoms affect their sexual drive. Together, you and your husband can find ways to ease these symptoms. The good news is that for many women, menopause can be a time of liberation—no more concerns about getting pregnant, and perhaps the children are out of the house, providing you and your husband more privacy.

Reflecting Our Lives

Those of us who have been married a while have come to realize that what goes on in the bedroom is reflective of what goes on in other areas of our lives. Intimacy involves not only giving our bodies to our husbands; it involves giving our hearts as well. This means that we must be vulnerable with our husbands: letting them know our feelings, our fears, our hopes and our dreams, even our weaknesses and sins. It is difficult to be close sexually if we are resistant or withdrawn in the daily walks of life. How can we wholeheartedly give ourselves sexually if we are unwilling to let our husbands know who we really are? When we are open and humble with our husbands, then truly, "The two shall become one" (Ephesians 5:31).

Together for Life

One of the greatest things about being committed to one man for life is that we can be patient with each other. Whatever the challenges and difficulties, we have a lifetime to deal with them and to be healed. In every marriage, there will undoubtedly be sexual interludes that are a bit flat. Our patience helps us to understand when our spouse is tired, ill, edgy or really not in the mood. This is not the end of the world! Sometimes, sex may be a "fireworks" experience of ecstasy. Sometimes sex may be a warm, glowing and comfortable feeling. Other times sex may be disappointing when things don't go at all as planned. Still other times sex is a time of fun and laughter. In every instance let us reaffirm, "We are committed to intimacy; we are bonded for life."

Each stage of marriage is so special, so unique. Newlyweds have everything before them; everything is new and exciting. Those who have a few years behind them have grown close; they have learned how to live together, how to adjust and adapt. Those with children have the joy of watching the results of their union—their children—grow and develop their own personalities. Older couples have experienced joy and grief, sickness and health, trials and victories. Each one of these stages has an impact on the sexual relationship between husband and wife. Each stage can draw the married couple into deeper intimacy. That is the way God designed it.

Now, it is time for me to stop talking about this subject, and do something about it. And I suggest you do the same.

INTO YOUR HEART

1. Reread the three scriptures at the beginning of this chapter. Then write down the way each affects you. What is the primary truth you learn from them?

2. Think back to your honeymoon. What were the high points? The low points? What did you learn about each other? Think about how much you have grown in your knowledge since then.

3. Are there some things that are taking the fire out of your sexual relationship with your husband? What are you personally going to do to fan the flames?

4. How do you feel about having variety in your sex life? How does your husband feel?

5. How vulnerable are you willing to be with your husband (on a scale of one to ten)? How do you think this willingness or lack thereof affects your sexual intimacy?

6. Do you have any "trust issues" that hurt your marriage and especially the sexual relationship? If so, who will you get help from to resolve these? Are you willing to let go of the lack of trust?

7. Write any other response to this chapter and commitments you want to make.

1. Oneness, Commitment, lifetime.
Marriage is a commitment throughout
my lifetime. "... may you rejoice in the
wife of your youth... May her breasts
satisfy you always." (lifetime)
- Song of Solomon 2:3-6
My lover is like the apple tree in the
forest; provides fruit (edible), provides
shade, overpowering, big, strong bark.
My lover strengthens + refreshes.
I need to have a mindset that his
fruit is sweet to my taste. Right now,
I don't think so. It makes me feel
nauseous + gag. There is joy + love.
- Prov 5:19. I spend the rest of
my life w/ Collin.
- Eph 5:31-32. I become one.
The purpose of me is to become one -
united. (Oneness w/ Collin).
physically, emotionally, spiritually, in
thought, in complementing as other ♡

119

2. Honeymoon

High Point - Being w/ Collin 4 the 1st time;
being w/ anyone 4 the first time.
- Seeing how God has brought me this
far, this close. How God allowed
everything to fall into place ~ the
friendship; nothing going wrong,
God being revealed & glorified.
- Just being w/ Collin + exploring.
- " " able to spend time w/
Collin + not having to look at the time ~
unrushed time.
- Have fun; being close to Collin

★ Low Point - When I made Collin
feel burdened by him feeling nothing
he does is ever enough. At airport
returning home. (Prov 21:9)
Collin will do anything for me to be happy.

♡

120

Sexual Specifics

♡ *GEB*

> "Probably no one else has this problem."
> "Something must be wrong with me."
> "No one would understand."
> "This is too embarrassing to talk about." ✓
> "I wonder if our sexual relationship is normal."
> "We agreed not to talk about this."

Do any of these statements sound like thoughts you have had? You are not unusual if these or similar thoughts have crossed your mind. The main problem with sexual questions is our tendency to keep them to ourselves. By not being open we block the very help we need. Without input from the right sources our questions and problems loom bigger and bigger in our own eyes. We need to appreciate the people God has put in our lives—our disciplers, mature Christian couples, Christian doctors and counselors—and make the most of their wisdom. While it is true that each couple is unique, our problems are not so different.

Physical, Mental, Emotional, Spiritual

Every aspect of our being will affect our sexual experience:

- Physical: Are you healthy or sick? Energetic or fatigued?
- Mental: What do you know about the sexual relationship? What are your thoughts about sex?
- Emotional: How do you feel about yourself and others as sexual beings?
- Spiritual: What are your beliefs about God and his view of sex?

In looking for solutions to sexual problems, it is essential to recognize the multifaceted influences on an individual's view of sex. This consideration helps us to understand why the brain has been called the most vital sex organ.

Gary Chapman in his book *The Five Love Languages* states, "Most sexual problems in marriage have little to do with physical technique but everything to do with meeting emotional needs." He gives more details to help understand some of the basic differences between men and women:

> For the male, sexual desire is physically based. That is, the desire for sexual intercourse is stimulated by the buildup of sperm cells and seminal fluid in the seminal vesicles. When the seminal vesicles are full,

there is a physical push for release. Thus, the male's desire for sexual intercourse has a physical root. For the female, sexual desire is rooted in her emotions, not her physiology. There is nothing physically that builds up and pushes her to have intercourse. Her desire is emotionally based. If she feels loved and admired and appreciated by her husband, then she has a desire to be physically intimate with him. But without the emotional closeness she may have little physical desire. [1]

Different Frequency Needs

Early in our marriage Al and I realized that our sex drives were different. There were times when I thought that sex was all he thought about; there were times when I thought there was something wrong with me; and there were times when I thought everything was perfect. As we matured in our relationship and began counseling other couples, we realized that many couples experience differing levels of sexual need. Most often it was the man who had the greater need, but sometimes it was the woman. When this is the case, the woman should not think something is wrong with her. God has just given her a strong sex drive.

In general, we counsel couples to come to a mutual decision that the frequency of lovemaking should be determined by the one with the greater need. Marriage exposes our selfishness like no other relationship. If we hold on to a selfish concern for meeting our own needs rather than being sure we are meeting our husbands' needs, there will be problems. Paul gives this godly perspective in 1 Corinthians 7:3-5:

> The husband should fulfill his marital duty to his wife, and likewise the wife to her husband. The wife's body does not belong to her alone but also to her husband. In the same way, the husband's body does not belong to him alone but also to his wife. Do not deprive each other except by mutual consent and for a time, so that you may devote yourselves to prayer. Then come together again so that Satan will not tempt you because of your lack of self-control.

God has given husbands and wives the unique privilege and responsibility of fulfilling their partners' sexual needs. Other avenues of fulfillment are not God's plan. I came to realize that though Al has the stronger sex drive, I need our sexual relationship as much as he does. While I appreciate and enjoy the physical satisfaction, I primarily need the emotional closeness and what it does for our communication.

John Gray in *Mars and Venus in the Bedroom* gives this analogy:

> Women are like the moon. Sometimes she is in the full-moon stage of her cycle, sometimes she is in the half-moon stage, and sometimes she is in the new-moon stage....Men are like the sun. Every morning, it rises with a big smile![2]

We might as well laugh and enjoy our differences. It is a good thing that the husband's hormone levels do not fluctuate as his wife's do. Wives, we need to be alert to our cyclic changes and take godly control of our emotions, not using them as an excuse to sin. The challenge is to have an unselfish "give and take" attitude to lovingly meet each other's needs.

I have found that one of the most vital times to give unselfishly in the sexual relationship is right after you have worked through a conflict. There seems to be an awkwardness at that time since the feelings may still be a little raw. It has been amazing to me to see how much more easily and quickly we get back "on track" with each other when I initiate lovemaking at these times. Some wives may balk at this because they would feel hypocritical. On the contrary, you are being faithful to God because you are taking hold of your own emotions and not allowing your feelings to control you. With the right attitude and actions, the loving feelings soon return. God blesses unselfish giving.

Pressure to Perform

An obstacle to great sex can be the focus on orgasm as the goal of the sexual relationship. While orgasm is certainly an important goal, it is not the only measure of the quality of your sex life. For some women achieving an orgasm is difficult. In a small percentage of women the problem may be a physical one, but generally the problem has to do with the woman's emotions and thoughts. If sex becomes so goal oriented, undue pressure can be put on both the husband and the wife. It would be sad to focus so much on the "destination" that you failed to enjoy the "journey."

One of the most helpful hints to the wife is to relax and enjoy. As Kay mentioned in chapter 7, we have a lifetime to learn how to please and pleasure each other as husband and wife. It is important to remember that it takes more time for the woman to be aroused to a point of climax. Even in today's world where sex is talked about so openly, it is possible for couples to be uneducated about their bodies. Reading together some of the books listed at the end of this book could be very rewarding. It helps to understand such things as the importance of adequate lubrication, which strokes or movements feel best, and the fact that almost all female orgasms result from the stimulation of the clitoris. Times of "show and tell" are important to help educate each other about what feels good. Wives should not expect their husbands to be mind readers...and an added bonus is that a wife's guiding of her husband is often exciting to him!

Although orgasm is not the only goal of lovemaking, it is still a very pleasurable culmination. It is especially vital for the wife to realize how important it is to her husband to be able to bring her to completion in an orgasm. A large part of his fulfillment as a husband and lover is fulfilling his wife. The husband also needs to realize that his wife may not need an orgasm as frequently as he does, and that satisfying him in a "quickie" at times can also fulfill her.

Expectations

Expectations in and of themselves are not a problem. The fact that so many of our expectations are not communicated *is* a problem. We all had our ideas and dreams of what our sexual relationship would be like when we married. Depending on our backgrounds and experiences, these ideas could have been passionate or prudish or anything in between. Difficulties will be encountered if the passionate marries the prudish. One young bride I counseled was appalled at the thought of touching her husband's penis. The husband expected each time of intercourse to be "skyrockets" for both him and his wife. Imagine the confusion and disappointment that resulted from their uncommunicated thoughts and expectations.

Expectations also need to be educated. Back in the early days of our marriage the topic of oral sex was never discussed (although we had discovered it!). Times have changed. One commentator recently stated that fifty years ago the risqué side of dating involved French kissing, but today it is oral sex. Sadly, the younger generation is sinfully experimenting while some of the older marrieds may not have discovered oral sex. Several years ago a couple came to talk with Al and me about this topic. The husband enjoyed his wife pleasuring him, but he was hesitant to reciprocate. We shared some verses from God's poetic sex manual that seem to allude to oral sex:

Like an apple tree among the trees of the forest
  is my lover among the young men.
I delight to sit in his shade,
  and his fruit is sweet to my taste.
(Song of Songs 2:3)

Let my lover come into his garden
and taste its choice fruits. (Song of Songs 4:16)

Talking openly with another Christian couple and searching for God's answers certainly helps educate our expectations. The couple I mentioned has thanked us many times for that talk.

Since lovemaking is to be a mutually pleasing experience for the husband and wife, it needs to be said that one would not want to violate the other's conscience or do anything that would be offensive to him or her.

Overcoming Obstacles

There are stages and events in our lives that radically affect our sexual relationships. Sam and Geri Laing cover many of these problem areas in their book *Friends and Lovers*.[3] My intention here is to cover a few of the areas and give some helps and thoughts from women who have gone through the various experiences.

During Pregnancy and After Childbirth

Don't forget your husband; his body and his needs haven't changed just because you are pregnant or recovering from childbirth. Be creative in satisfying him—try some new positions or manual stimulation. Oral sex is also an option. Think more about admiring his body than worrying about how your body looks. Express a lot of appreciation. Don't expect him to respond exactly like you do to the new baby. His emotions will be different from yours; that is good. Someone needs to steady the ship!

Painful Intercourse

A brand new wife, a mom who has just given birth or a woman with certain medical problems might experience painful intercourse. This can be a source of heartache and confusion. A visit to the doctor is needed for accurate diagnosis so proper help can be given. As with other problems, it is important to have a mature Christian woman with whom you can be open. Whatever the circumstances, it helps if your husband is patient and loving. Let him know what you need from him and talk openly with a strong couple to get support.

Grief

Different people handle grief in different ways. Years ago we knew a woman who lost her mother and was so devastated emotionally that she and her husband did not have sex for almost a year! That is extreme. Another woman, after losing her mother, made the decision to put her parents' picture in another room rather than the bedroom so she would not be overcome with sadness when making love to her husband. After we lost our babies, Al and I needed each other for comfort and strength; it was a time that brought us closer. After I lost my mom and later my dad, I had to consciously share with Al the times I was sad so he could know my feelings. That helped me emotionally, and I was able to still give to him sexually although it was not my most responsive time. His understanding and patience helped my loving feelings return more quickly.

Husband's Adultery

While devastated after her husband's adultery, one wife made the decision not to give up, but to forgive her husband and work on their marriage. Her faith was built up through reading and applying scriptures such as Philippians 4:4-13, Proverbs 3:5-7, Psalm 23 and 2 Corinthians 10:5. She prayed and trusted God to erase her fears and insecurities especially during lovemaking. The sensitivity of her husband helped improve their communication. She listened to the people God put in her life. With God's help she retrained her heart and mind to have spiritual perspective...and sexual desire.

Wife's Adultery

A guilty wife learned the necessity of being broken before God and her husband. Her perspective radically changed as she saw things clearly—there was no truth in the sinful relationship, only guilt, shame and the lies of Satan. She learned to appreciate the true friendship of marriage. God's design became evident as she worked to make her husband her best friend. Her husband did his best not to bring up the past. He determined to forgive her and love her unconditionally. The truth really set them free to see God's blessings and the beauty of their sexual relationship like never before. By God's grace their marriage is better than ever.

Memories of Sexual Abuse

Recognize that your perspective of sex and intimacy has been distorted by your experience. Your husband is not the perpetrator and is not your enemy. Free yourself to enjoy intimacy again by changing perspective. Don't kill your longings but identify them. Your longings to have a close relationship and to be worthy of love can be fulfilled by God's power. Fight for intimacy with God and with your husband. Don't minimize your experience. Discipline your thoughts to replace the hurtful images with healthy, godly visions. Be open and be willing to get help as needed. Be prepared to face the hurts of the past in order to be released from their hold.

Sexually Transmitted Diseases (STDs)

Overcome guilt, shame and embarrassment. Accept God's forgiveness, yet realize the consequences of sin. Be open. Talk through times of outbreak. Be aware of heightened emotions. Be calm through prayer and meditation on God's word. Take care of your overall health. And remember that through Christ you are God's pure daughter.

Lack of Attraction for Husband

Remember that love is a decision. Watch out for self-talk such as "I don't know why I married him" or "I just don't have feelings for him." It is important to remember that feelings ebb and flow throughout a marriage; the commitment to one another is for life. Fill your mind with his positive traits. Say positive things to him and express appreciation for little things. Deal with any resentment that comes up so it does not turn into deep-seated bitterness. Pray for God to rekindle your love and responsiveness to your husband. Get help from a strong Christian couple so you can be open about needed changes.

Problem-Free Philosophy

The idea of a problem-free life sounds good in the song "Hakuna Matata" from the *Lion King*, but unfortunately life will have its problems—and problems will find their way into our bedrooms. Thankfully, God has grace and mercy on all of us, and he provides ways for us to deal with any problems we face. Of course, we have to choose to face them God's way. Many of us as women find that we naturally tend to be controlled by our feelings and emotions, especially when it comes to our sexuality. An amorous feeling can be snatched away from us in a split second by an angry tone or sharp word. Only as we commit ourselves to God's righteousness will we be able to overcome the strong pull of our emotions. We must make firm decisions to let go of resentment, bitterness and fear. We must accept God's forgiveness ourselves and then willingly forgive our husbands and others who may have sinned against us. Move past the past—don't mess up each new day with yesterday. God wants our marriages to be full of beauty, excitement, fulfillment and celebration.

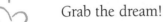 Grab the dream!

NOTES

1. Gary Chapman, *Five Love Languages* (Chicago: Northfield Publishing, 1995), 121.

2. John Gray, *Mars and Venus in the Bedroom* (New York: Harper Perennial, 1951), 66.

3. Sam and Geri Laing, *Friends and Lovers* (Billerica, Mass.: Discipleship Publications International, 1996).

INTO YOUR HEART

1. Look at the six statements that begin this chapter. Have you ever thought any of these? If so, have you been open with anyone about those thoughts? If not, why not?

2. In what way does your sexual relationship with your husband reflect your emotional relationship with him?

3. Which of you tends to want more variety and "adventure" in your sexual relationship? If you are the one, have you expressed your desires to your husband, and are you willing to be patient with him in this area? If he is the one, have you been willing to go out of your comfort zone to spice up your lovemaking? If not, why not?

4. Is there any specific problem area in your sexual relationship right now? Have the two of you discussed it, prayed about it, gotten help and formulated a plan?

5. What commitment do you want to specifically make to your husband for your sexual relationship? Write it down and (gulp!) share it with him.

6. Write any other response to this chapter and commitments you want to make.

And Baby Makes Three, Four, Five...

♡ *KSM*

> We used to talk of so many things,
> Roses and summer and golden rings,
> Music and dances and books and plays,
> Venice and moonlight and future days.
>
> Now our chief subjects are food and bills,
> Genevieve's measles and Johnny's ills;
> New shoes for Betty, a hat for Jane,
> Taxes, insurance, the mail and rain!
>
> We used to say that Romance would stay.
> We'd walk together in a magic way!
> Though we don't talk as in days of yore,
> Strange, is it not, that I love you more?[1]
> —Anne Campbell

My hands were trembling as I answered the phone. It was the doctor's office telling me the result of the blood test. "It's positive," she said.

I wanted to be absolutely sure that I understood her. "What does that mean?" I asked.

"It means you are pregnant."

I hung up the phone and walked down the hall to where my husband sat at his desk. One look at my face and he knew. We could not decide whether to laugh or to cry. Only one thing we knew for sure: *This changes everything!*

Bringing a baby into this world does change everything, and it especially changes the relationship between a husband and wife. No longer is the relationship about them alone, but about another human being, a person who will be dependent upon them, who will need them, who will bring out the best and worst in them individually and as a couple. This experience does not just affect the short years that the child is in the home, but it affects a lifetime. It is joy and sorrow, victory and defeat, tears and laughter, pain and pleasure. Best of all, it is something a man and a woman go through *together*.

It is obvious that conceiving a child takes the union of two people, but raising a child calls for a unity that is even deeper. Once this new human being is cradled in his mother's arms, a new kind of love arises in her heart; it is fierce and primal. It is a love so protective and exclusive that many new mothers inadvertently leave their husbands out of the picture. A wife needs to always remember that her child needs his father—but equally important is the fact that she needs his father as well.

Jesus said, "You who are evil know how to give good gifts to your children" (Matthew 7:11). He knew that even though we have our sins and faults, we truly want to give the best we have to our kids. There are so many things we want to make sure our children have: a good education, the best health care, opportunities to develop their talents, financial security, a solid church ministry—on and on the list goes. But there are two things that are of the greatest value that we must strive to bestow upon our children: first, the gift of faith in a loving God, and second, the gift of assurance that Mom and Dad love each other.

Our relationship with our husbands should be a safe haven for the children. There can be no greater security than knowing that Mom and Dad share a commitment to honor, love and respect each another for the rest of their lives. Children have enough fears in their lives to deal with—fear of pain, fear of strangers, fear of the unknown. We should not add to those fears by making them insecure about the only really solid thing they have on earth: their family. Even though my children know that I am not perfect and that their father is not perfect, I am confident that they know we love each other! Better yet, they know that we like each other, have fun together, and are best friends.

In the midst of child-rearing years, when there can be financial stress, sleepless nights, visits to doctors and calls from the principal's office, it is very difficult to keep rekindling the romance between husband and wife. I certainly never felt very amorous with spit up running down my blouse and dirty diapers in my hands. Even when we could find a babysitter and save up money for a night out, it seemed those were the times that a child's temperature shot up to 102 degrees, or a fall off the bike meant a trip to the hospital for stitches. How can you relax at a nice restaurant when your child is on the cell phone with the latest crisis? Even if we do have the courage to turn off the phone, we can never "turn off" being parents, can we?

Good Times

It is ideal to plan time away occasionally from the children—a few nights when the kids are with a trusted friend or family member or just a few hours to get time to talk and be alone. Be creative to plan this with your husband, to remind him that he is still special to you and that you value him. However, even when the little ones are underfoot, you can still be a wife that exudes love and affection for your husband. Little endearments keep drawing you together: kisses when you meet at the end of a hard day, hugs and touches as you go about the home, winks and smiles as the children are babbling on about who knows what.

Remind the children to thank their father for things he does: "Let's all say thank you to Daddy for taking us to McDonald's!" "Isn't Daddy strong to carry you on his shoulders?" Every day with your family is a future memory for your children. What will they remember about their parents? Will they have fond thoughts of fun, consideration and respect? Will they know that you are their father's #1 fan? Their impression of you and your husband will be lodged in their hearts for years to come. It will make a huge difference in how they view themselves, how they view other people and how they view marriage. Again, this is not to say that they need to see you as faultless, but rather they need to see parents who are doing the best they can and who are loving each other in the process.

These precious bundles of joy will, eventually, grow up and leave the nest. What will they leave behind? If you are so consumed with the children that you forget their father, then one day you will be staring at a stranger across the dinner table. Never forget to invest time and energy and money into the man who is your husband. Do all you can to nurture your relationship with him.

One other hint: It doesn't hurt to keep a lock on your bedroom door!

Not So Good Times

Children are precious. They are an extension of their parents—they have their father's eyes, their mother's nose; their father's athletic abilities, their mother's sense of humor. They make us laugh with their jokes and stories, and they impress us with their capabilities and insights. We love to talk about their escapades, even when they embarrass us to no end. I laughed at the episode I heard about a little boy who was acting up in church. The parents were trying to calm him down but to no avail. Finally the father picked the little guy up and carried him firmly up the aisle to the exit. Just before they reached the door, the boy called out loudly to everyone in the congregation: "Pray for me! Pray for me!" These are the times that parents want to crawl under their chairs and not come out for a few years.

While we can chuckle about the little bouts of misbehavior that all children go through, we also cry about the genuine struggles and trials that we must face with our children, especially adolescents. When our sweet little girls and boys display characters that are displeasing to us as parents, it can test us as mothers; it can also test us as wives. How will we behave toward our husbands when the kids are going through trying times? Since there is nothing so dear to our hearts as our children, nothing so tender or fragile as our feelings for them, it is easy to let these difficult times cause tension in our marriages. Sadly, the times when couples should cling to one another for help and support often become the times of blaming and accusing each other.

Everyone makes their share of mistakes in raising children. There is not one parent who can say, "I have done all things well." We are painfully aware of this when troubles arise with our children—but that does not give us the right to point the finger at our spouses! This is the opportunity to draw closer together, give encouragement and comfort each another. Instead of adding to the problems by being angry with your husband for a mistake he made as a father, it is important to remind yourself and remind your child that Mom and Dad are in this together. It may be right and good to gently point out what you see that could ease a conflict between your husband and your child, but even then the child should know that his parents are united, and no man—or child—is going to separate them!

Thankfully, God also blesses us with "fellow warriors" in this parenting adventure—brothers and sisters in the church who have gone through similar challenges and are eager to help and support us. We should never neglect to get the help we need from other couples. Proverbs 15:22 teaches us that "plans fail for lack of counsel, but with many advisers they succeed." If we can develop openness with other Christians, they will enable us to make the best decisions as a couple and as parents. Our children are blessed when they know that even Mom and Dad are humble enough to get help from others.

Being a parent is the most challenging job in this world. Raising a child to become a productive and responsible adult takes tears, effort, sweat, blood and a multitude of prayers. What a joy to know that we do not have to do it alone. Your husband is there with you, and he wants the same thing that you want: whatever is best for your child. You may not agree on everything, but you know that you both love your children deeply and would die for them. Your husband is your partner, your collaborator, your colleague, your friend, your shoulder to cry on and your pal to celebrate with. Yes, having a child in the family does change everything. It changes everything for the better...when you do it together!

NOTES

1. *Poems That Touch The Heart*, (Garden City, New York: Doubleday and Company, 1963), 287.

INTO YOUR HEART

1. If you have children, think back to each time you found out you were pregnant. How did you feel?

2. Have you identified the tendency to neglect your husband's needs because you are so focused on meeting your children's needs? If you are not sure, ask him. If you are sure, ask him.☺

3. In what special ways do you make sure you are staying connected with your husband emotionally in your busy household? How does your effort to stay connected with him affect your children?

4. In what ways do you feel challenged in meeting your husband's needs? Share your answer with a spiritual friend and get her input.

5. How has having children brought you and your husband closer together?

6. Write any other response to this chapter and commitments you want to make.

Enjoying the Empty Nest

> Think about it. No more Christmas presents out of tooth-picks and library paste. No more sloppy, oatmeal kisses. No more tooth fairy. Only a voice crying, "Why don't you grow up?" and the silence echoing, "I did."
>
> —Erma Bombeck

The story is told of a woman who attempted to write a script for her life. No matter what she wrote, she was not content with it. She crumpled page after page, tossing each into the wastebasket. She spent so much time trying to figure out just the perfect script that she never even got around to living her life…and she ended up with a wastebasket filled with crumpled paper.

What a waste of time and energy it is when we fail to enjoy our life day by day, stage by stage!

One of the reasons we older women can train the younger women is that we have already lived through a number of life's stages. Certainly this gives us a unique perspective—we have hindsight. The fact that we have lived through these stages is proof that others can live through them too. The question is, how will you move through the stages of your life? Again, your attitude is the key factor in shaping your view of life and its many shifts and turns. (See chapter 6.)

I have heard women almost doom their empty-nest years with statements such as "I dread the time when all the kids leave home" or "It will be unbearably lonely with no kids around" or "My husband and I will have nothing to do but stare at each other." It is vital to remember how much your thinking affects your attitude and how much your attitude affects your husband, children and everyone around you.

Making the Preparations

Remember how you felt on your child's first day of school? You were preparing for the empty nest. How did you react the first time your child spent the night away from you? You were getting ready for the empty nest. Has your child graduated from high school? Gone to college? These times in life are steps in your preparation for the empty nest. How you go through these steps will determine whether you enjoy your empty nest or not.

Years ago I was encouraged to "untie the apron strings" as opposed to "cutting the apron strings." I prefer a gradual untying rather than an abrupt cutting.

When the children leave home it may seem like an abrupt event, but in reality it is a process that occurs over time. One of the goals of your parenting is to prepare your child to meet the responsibilities of life as an adult. You do not want them holding on to your apron strings; you do not want a "Mama's boy." You want to help them grow up and mature. In fact, you might say one of your major life goals is to effectively empty your nest!

In preparing for the stage of marriage when it is back to the two of you—husband and wife—your husband must have his rightful place all along. From the birth of your first baby, the needs and activities of the children vie for your husband's #1 spot. A wife too easily assumes that her husband can take care of himself since he is an adult. God's plan in marriage is that it starts and ends with just the husband and the wife: "For this reason a man will leave his father and mother and be united to his wife, and they will become one flesh" (Genesis 2:24).

Your husband is the only one who will stay with you for life; the kids will leave. Keeping that principle in mind will help you keep your priorities right. A statement I make to wives is "You love your children better when you love your husband best." Your children need to see that their mom and dad come first with each other, second only to God. Not only is that a godly model for them, but also it gives them security.

When children leave home, the mother may wonder, "Who am I now?" Whether you have been a career mom or a stay-at-home mom or both, much of your life has been spent caring for your children—cooking, cleaning, driving, training. Then suddenly you have worked yourself out of a job! Nothing helps more in the preparation for this transition time than the realization that as women of God, disciples of Jesus, our purpose in life is to please God and help others learn to please him too. Some of our roles and activities may change, but we can fulfill our God-given purpose in every stage of our lives.

Dealing with the Feelings

Sad...lonely...nostalgic...depressed...aching. These are some of the feelings I had as our girls left home. And yes, *empty*! There is a reason this stage of life is often referred to as the empty nest. Of course, there were other feelings mixed in: pride...accomplishment...love...gratitude. This mixture of feelings is the dilemma for most of us—we are not sure what we are feeling. In a sense we need to mourn the loss of the previous stage of life. It does feel like a loss. On the other hand, we know we should be happy and grateful. My tendency is to "keep a stiff upper lip" and be strong, but I have found that the emotions and feelings will come out one way or the other.

My most vivid memory of dealing with my empty-nest feelings happened when Al and I were riding in a car with Bob and Pat Gempel. My emotions caught up with me and the tears began to flow. I remember saying that I didn't know what I was feeling, but as I talked, the feelings became obvious. Bob was able to clarify the situation: Staci had moved to London, Kristi was traveling with Kip and Elena McKean, and Keri had moved to L.A. At the same time we had sold the house we had lived in for twenty years and were living in temporary housing. Not only had our nest been emptied; we no longer had our nest.

One of the most important lessons I learned at that time was how necessary it is to be open and to talk about what I am feeling. Years later, I still have to remember that lesson and apply it. Even though our nest has been empty for a number of years, some of the feelings recur. This past Christmas was special for Al and me as we temporarily filled our nest to overflowing with thirteen from our family. With five little granddaughters we had lots of fun, action, laughter, tears—lots of everything. As they were leaving, four-year-old Kaleigh asked me, "Nonna, are you going to cry when we leave?"

I responded with, "I'm going to feel like crying, but I'm not going to cry. I'm going to remember all the fun we had."

Yeah, sure! Guess who was swallowing hard, fighting back the tears. And then crying several times after they all left? In fact, I could not get a grip on my emotions until I opened up with Al and talked about what I was feeling.

I once heard a concise statement about dealing with emotions: you express them then you dismiss them. In other words, do not let your emotions and feelings control you. God's way is for us to pour out our hearts to him (Psalm 62:8) and to open wide our hearts to each other (2 Corinthians 6:13).

The early experiences of separation—such as your child's first day of school—give a glimmer of things to come. It is just a glimmer because your nest is empty for only a few hours; your child is only gone temporarily. The permanent "empty" goes a lot deeper. The way you handle these temporary transitions will determine how you handle the permanent ones. Have you learned to deal with your fears and worries? Have you learned to obey 2 Corinthians 10:5 and "take captive every thought to make it obedient to Christ"? After expressing your feelings, have you determined to focus on the positive and be thankful? Making these decisions and acting on them with God's help will set you up to enjoy your empty nest.

Relishing the Good Part

Al and I say we are now "old enough" to appreciate having just the two of us in the house. We jokingly say honeymoons are wasted on the youngsters. There is an extra freedom to our lifestyle that we could not have when the kids were at home. (Some of those freedoms are best left to the imagination.) We no longer have to plan our lives around school schedules or extracurricular activities. The number of kids in the neighborhood and the quality of the local school system do not have to be considered when we are looking for a place to live. It is easier to move an empty nest than a full one— and we have certainly tested this theory. We can take a trip at the drop of a hat since we do not need to find someone to stay with the kids or find places for them to stay.

Through the years we have shared so many experiences that have deepened our relationship in unique ways. Some of those experiences have been exhilarating, heartwarming and hysterically funny. Others have been challenging, heartbreaking and sad.

We learned in our early years of marriage how bonding the birth of a child can be. There is an excitement at the safe arrival of a baby that the mother and father share uniquely, no matter how many people are celebrating with them.

In contrast, when you lose a baby (Al and I lost three), there is a depth of sorrow and pain that only the parents can share. As we have gone through various joys and sorrows, victories and tragedies, and as we have watched others do the same, we have learned that we can choose to be pulled closer to each other and God or to be pulled away from each other and God.

Looking back at the hard times in our lives, we see how much God keeps his promises, as in Romans 8:28: "And we know that in all things God works for the good of those who love him, who have been called according to his purpose." Our faith has been strengthened as we have seen God work through the "ebb and flow" of life—his constancy through the changes.

In the midst of difficult situations I try to remember that today is not the whole of my life; there will also be good times and blessings from God. The empty-nest stage is a time to look for the joys of life and to keep a good sense of humor. Grandchildren must be God's answer for that! One of the greatest blessings in our lives is seeing our children with their children, loving and serving God. After a hard day I am amazed at how quickly our spirits can be lifted by a phone call from one of our granddaughters. They surely light up our lives!

New Opportunities

It is important to have some common interests to share with your husband. Certainly grandchildren and family should be a big part of that, but it is worth the effort to find some activities that you and your husband can enjoy together. Al and I are in the beginning stages of golfing; we both love to go snorkeling; we go for walks on the beach and try to work out frequently. A vital part of staying young (at least young at heart) is to be a continual learner. A goal for me this year is to learn more about the computer. Al is a great teacher and I am having lots of fun learning.

Working together can also be a great source of joy. For some that may mean working on a project around the house, gardening or working in the ministry together. Al and I consider it a great privilege and one of God's best gifts to work side by side on the ministry staff helping people to know and walk with God. Our work enriches this stage of our lives like nothing else.

Another benefit of the empty nest is that it has room for other people. Since our girls left home we have had many different people live with us. We have had families, couples, singles and children with us for various lengths of time and for various reasons. Each person has added to our lives and has made our nest better. I will forever be grateful that we were able to have my dad with us before he died at age ninety. Al and I were able to work together as a team, along with my brother and sister-in-law, to care for him. Al's willingness and eagerness to serve my dad in such selfless ways deepened my love and respect for him—it strengthened our empty nest.

Full, not Empty

Whatever stage of life you are in, God wants you to enjoy it. Jesus said in John 10:10, "I have come that they may have life, and have it to the full." He was not just talking about one stage of life. Keeping our focus on God's plan and his work will help us with our priorities. Making daily choices that follow Jesus' example will keep us on the right path. A day-to-day walk with God adds up to a stage-by-stage walk with God...and life to the full!

The key to enjoying the empty nest is to enjoy the full one. I don't know about you, but we are having the time of our lives—but then that is what we said when we were newlyweds.

INTO YOUR HEART

1. If you are not in the empty-nest phase of life yet, how do you need to be preparing for it?

2. If this phase of life is just around the corner for you, are you being open with your husband and others about any fears you might have? What are those fears?

3. What are some of the bonding experiences you and your husband have had that will help you stay emotionally close when the children have left the nest?

4. If you are in the empty-nest phase, are you allowing yourself to thoroughly enjoy it? What new activities can you try, or what new adventures can you embark upon?

5. Is your life as an "empty nester" appealing to those coming behind you? As a disciple, how should and can it be?

6. Write any other response to this chapter and commitments you want to make.

Helpful Books

The majority of the material in the following books is helpful and Biblical.

Friends and Lovers, Sam and Geri Laing (Discipleship Publications International)

The Five Love Languages, Dr. Gary Chapman (Northfield Publishing)

Night Light: A Devotional for Couples, Dr. James and Shirley Dobson (Multnomah Publishers)

The Act of Marriage, Tim and Beverly LaHaye (Zondervan)

The Gift of Sex, Clifford and Joyce Penner (Word Publishing)

Intended for Pleasure, Ed and Gaye Wheat (Fleming H. Revell Company)

Intimate Issues: Conversations Woman to Woman—21 Questions Christian Women Ask About Sex, Linda Dillow and Lorraine Pintus (WaterBrook Press)

Love Life for Every Married Couple, Ed Wheat, M.D. and Gloria Okes Perkins (Zondervan)

A Celebration of Sex: A Guide to Enjoying God's Gift of Married Sexual Pleasure, Dr. Douglas E. Rosenau (Nelson)

About the Authors

Gloria Elaine Baird holds a bachelor's degree in elementary education from the University of Texas. She became a Christian in Boston in 1986 and began to train for the full-time ministry. She and her husband, Al, led the Boston Church of Christ and helped to establish churches throughout the Middle East. Today, they oversee law and media relations for the International Churches of Christ. Gloria and Al have been married thirty-nine years and are the parents of three daughters who serve with their husbands in the full-time ministry. They are also grandparents of six girls. The Bairds have taught marriage and parenting classes around the world and make their home in Los Angeles.

Kay Summers McKean graduated from the University of Florida with a degree in broadcast journalism from the College of Communications. She and her husband, Randy, have served in the full-time ministry in South Carolina, Florida, Japan and throughout Europe. The McKeans currently lead the Boston Church of Christ and are responsible for mission work with the International Churches of Christ in Continental Europe and New England. Kay and Randy have been married twenty-four years, and their two children, Summer and Kent, are also in the ministry. They have taught marriage and parenting classes around the world.

WHO ARE WE?

Discipleship Publications International (DPI) began publishing in 1993. We are a nonprofit Christian publisher affiliated with the International Churches of Christ, committed to publishing and distributing materials that honor God, lift up Jesus Christ and show how his message practically applies to all areas of life. We have a deep conviction that no one changes life like Jesus and that the implementation of his teaching will revolutionize any life, any marriage, any family and any singles household.

Since our beginning we have published more than 100 titles; plus we have produced a number of important, spiritual audio products. More than one million volumes have been printed, and our works have been translated into more than a dozen languages—international is not just a part of our name! Our books are shipped regularly to every inhabited continent.

To see a more detailed description of our works, find us on the World Wide Web at www.dpibooks.org. You can order books by calling 1-888-DPI-BOOK twenty-four hours a day. From outside the US, call 978-670-8840 during Boston-area business hours.

We appreciate the hundreds of comments we have received from readers. We would love to hear from you. Here are other ways to get in touch:

Mail: DPI, 2 Sterling Road, Billerica, Massachusetts 01862
E-mail: dpibooks@icoc.org

FIND US ON THE WORLD WIDE WEB

WWW.DPIBOOKS.ORG

1-888-DPI-BOOK

OUTSIDE US: 978-670-8840